SUTHERLAND QUARTERLY

SQ

Sutherland Quarterly is an exciting new series of captivating essays on current affairs by some of Canada's finest writers, published individually as books and also available by annual subscription.

SUBSCRIBE ONLINE AT
SUTHERLANDQUARTERLY.COM

FLEECED

FLEECED

Canadians Versus Their Banks

ANDREW SPENCE

SUTHERLAND HOUSE

Sutherland House
416 Moore Ave., Suite 304
Toronto, ON M4G 1C9

Copyright © 2024 by Andrew Spence

All rights reserved, including the right to reproduce this book or portions thereof in any form whatsoever. For information on rights and permissions or to request a special discount for bulk purchases, please contact Sutherland House at sutherlandhousebooks@gmail.com.

Sutherland House and logo are registered trademarks of The Sutherland House Inc.

First edition, September 2024

We acknowledge the support of the Government of Canada.

Manufactured in Canada
Cover designed by Shalomi Ranasinghe and Jordan Lunn

Library and Archives Canada Cataloguing in Publication
Title: Fleeced : Canadians versus their banks / Andrew Spence.
Names: Spence, Andrew (Economist), author.
Description: Series statement: Sutherland quarterly ; 7
Identifiers: Canadiana (print) 20240446461 | Canadiana (ebook) 2024044650X | ISBN 9781990823992 (softcover) | ISBN 9781998365043 (EPUB)
Subjects: LCSH: Banks and banking—Corrupt practices—Canada.
Classification: LCC HG2704 .S64 2024 | DDC 332.10971—dc23

ISBN 978-1-990823-99-2
eBook 978-1-998365-04-3

***Sutherland Quarterly*, Issue 7**
Editor – Ken Whyte
Managing Editor – Shalomi Ranasinghe
Associate Editor – Leah Ciani
Marketing Director – Serina Mercier
Publicist – Sarah Miniaci

Subscription Price: $67.99 CAD (includes HST) | Single Copy Price: $17.95 USD / $19.95 CAD

For submissions and more information, e-mail us at submissions@sutherlandhousebooks.com.

CONTENTS

Part One   1

Part Two   9

Part Three   19

Part Four   30

Part Five   36

Part Six   46

Part Seven   57

Part Eight   69

Part Nine   79

About the Author   89

PART ONE

Tucked away on page thirty-seven of the federal government's 2023 fall economic statement, amid other forgotten promises to make groceries, wireless services, and air travel more affordable for Canadians, was a commitment to crack down on "excess bank fees."

In particular, the government was disturbed that banks were charging consumers as much as $50 whenever an account had insufficient funds to cover a cheque or payment. The economic statement promised to do something about this at some point in the future, a promise repeated in the April 2024 budget and still not acted upon. It was nice of the government to at least recognize the problem, given that it created and regulates our banking system.

A few months after the economic statement was released, the research firm North Economics released a report showing that NSF (non-sufficient funds) fees in Canada are indeed between $45 and $48 *per instance*, compared to equivalent fees of between $0 and $5 in Australia and the United Kingdom, which have banking systems otherwise quite similar to ours.

NSF fees are the tip of the iceberg. Canadians are being gouged by their banks at every turn. Overdraft fees, for example. A Canadian typically has the choice between paying a $5 monthly fee to avoid overdraft charges or a $5 fee per instance. On top of those charges, customers pay interest rates of more than 20 percent on the amount they're overdrawn. Someone making three overdrafts a month for an amount of $1,000 will pay a total of either $111 (the $5 monthly fee) or $232 (the $5 per instance fee) in overdraft charges. A UK consumer will pay $77.

Chequing account fees are another way Canadian banks stick it to consumers. Only three in ten Canadians pay no service fees for their chequing accounts compared to 80 percent of Brits. And the Canadians who are paying no chequing account fees are generally those who can best afford to pay them: new Canadians, seniors, and students are unlikely to qualify for that particular break.

Any chance that we receive better service for those higher fees? Not at all. In the United Kingdom, cheques tend to clear within hours, and chequing accounts have daily transaction limits ranging between $30,000 and $170,000. In Canada, cheques tend to clear in four to eight business days, and daily transaction limits are typically $3,000 a day or $30,000 per thirty days. Canadians can speed things up by using the Interac e-Transfer system, but here again, the daily limits are low.

Canadian banks are in no hurry to see their customers switch from cheques to e-transfers because there are a lot of fees to be gobbled from chequing accounts. In fact, Canadians write five times as many cheques as Brits and ten times more than Australians.

The fees charged by banks for the use of automated teller machines (ATMs) are similarly appalling. It's generally free to use your own bank's ATMs, but should you need to use one at another bank, you'll usually pay between $3 and $6 for the privilege. Just under 80 percent of UK ATMs are free to use regardless of where you bank, while Australians pay a transaction fee of about $1.80 to use another bank's machines.

Canadian banks, by the way, jointly own the Interac ATM network. The average Interac charge to withdraw cash is $1.50, which is a trivial 0.15 percent fee when applied to a $1,000 transaction. However, for a $50.00 withdrawal, the fee is 3.0 percent. For $20, which many a cash-constrained individual might withdraw, the fee is a staggering 7.5 percent. Given the current return on a cash deposit, it would take about forty-six years of compounding to recover the fee for that one $20 transaction. Bear in mind that the additional cost to the bank of facilitating the $20 withdrawal is barely above zero.

A Canadian bank with $400 billion in consumer deposits will skim $4 billion from those accounts in fees, while a UK bank with the same amount on deposit will take only $2 billion in fees.

Our bankers are making out like bandits on the backs of consumers, and it's not like consumers have ready alternatives. The Canadian banking scene is dominated by six federally chartered banks. They all behave much the same way. One treats customers as abysmally as the others. It's not worth it for a consumer dissatisfied with his or her treatment at Royal Bank to cross the street to BMO, or TD, or Scotiabank, CIBC, or National Bank. The consumer who switches banks faces the administrative burden of moving accounts and assumes the risk of disrupting their credit relationship. Establishing credit is already challenging at Canada's conservative banks.

* * *

You might be thinking that small and medium businesses (SMBs) have it better. After all, they're the backbone of the Canadian economy, employing two-thirds of our private sector labour force. Our governments are always celebrating our independent business people. Banks, if their advertising is any indication, are eager to have independent businesses as clients. Surely the system works for them?

Again, not at all. What small businesses need most from banks is credit—loans to cover fluctuations in cash flow or to make new investments that will help them hire, expand, and grow. But banks do their best to avoid lending to small business people.

The Canadian Federation of Independent Business (CFIB) developed a guide for its members on how to navigate banks.

It made no bones about the fact that small businesses are likely to get a cool reception from their bankers. Entrepreneurial ventures, by their nature, involve risk. From the bank's perspective, the only good loan is the loan that gets paid back with certainty and interest. They hate risk. Mary Jane Grant, a consultant to CFIB, writes bluntly: "Understand from the outset that the banks are not in the risk business. They want to see a good base of equity investment, and they need assurance that loans can be repaid before they lend the money. They also want collateral..."

Banks insist on collateralized lending, which means that to get a bank loan, a small business must have already accumulated significant equity and must present collateral worth three times the value of the credit it seeks. To qualify, entrepreneurs and business leaders must pledge not just their home, but also a good chunk of the business value they've already built. That's a non-starter for a majority of independent business people.

Industry Canada reports there were 1,213,422 SMBs in Canada in 2023. Combined, they accounted for about half of Canada's gross domestic product, or GDP, a measure of all the goods and services produced in our country. Each business accounts for about $1,167,889 of value added. The CFIB survey of SMBs showed that the median amount of financing approved by a bank (outside of credit cards) was a mere $156,000 in 2022. This is for the firms that generate half of Canada's GDP!

Data compiled by the Organisation for Economic Co-operation and Development (OECD) also show that Canada's banks rank poorly in terms of credit provision. Ninety-eight percent of all businesses in Canada are small businesses, yet small businesses account for only $117.9 billion of the $1.007 trillion in debt held by all Canadian businesses in 2020, or 11.7 percent.

Unable to get bank loans, most businesses turn to alternative sources of financing, including loans from friends and family.

Or they divert a large share of their current earnings to growing the business, depriving themselves of an income. According to a 2015 survey commissioned by the CFIB, only one in five respondents accessed a bank loan or line of credit from a bank. Half of them financed themselves, tapping existing equity and personal lines of credit, and about 30 percent of them used their high-interest-rate credit cards. The steep cost of credit card financing transfers the entrepreneurial profit to the bank, leaving the entrepreneur with the risk.

There are even fewer options now than there were when the survey was taken. Of the 50 percent or so of small businesses that applied for bank financing, Canada's big banks accounted for about 40 percent of the total applications; the other 60 percent was to London-based HSBC and smaller lenders. Since then, lamentably, HSBC has opted to pull out of Canada. It sold out to RBC, sending chills down the spines of entrepreneurs relying on HSBC to achieve their goals.

If they do manage to get a bank loan, small businesses pay through the nose for it. The most recent 2023 Canadian Federation of Independent Business survey of the state of member financing showed that the financing spread over prime—prime is the rate given to the "best" borrowers—was more than 2 percent for small businesses, with the smallest businesses paying more than 2.5 percent. The spread between interest rates on loans to SMBs and those on loans to large corporations is a whopping 2.48 percent, compared to just 0.42 percent in the United States. Even Australia, which has a remarkably similar banking structure to Canada, has a significantly lower spread. The OECD also found that the number of SMB loans provided annually grew at just 2.4 percent and 5.5 percent, respectively, compared to overall loan growth of 9 percent.

This is a serious problem for Canada's economic growth, dynamism, and progress. Historically, our entrepreneurs have done their part. Every year, they step up to the plate with enthusiasm and create more than enough new businesses to replace those businesses that die. Even during the pandemic year of 2020, which brought the biggest economic shock in 100 years, Canada's entrepreneurs gave birth to 72,920 new businesses and said goodbye to 68,820, resulting in a net gain of 5,990. More recent signs, however, are troubling.

Since the pandemic, the annual growth rate in small businesses with just one to ninety-nine employees has ground to a halt at just one-third of 1 percent per year. Large firms have recovered to grow at 1.3 percent.

The 2023 CFIB financing survey shows that the median bank financing for SMBs is down significantly between 2012 and 2022. The aforementioned figure of $156,000 per business represents a 28 percent decline since 2012, when it was $217,600. To make matters worse, inflation has accelerated, with prices up 24.4 percent over the same period, reducing the real value of the financing by almost half. At the same time, nominal GDP has grown by 45 percent. If the median financing amount had kept pace with GDP, the median loan would now be $316,193, or more than double the 2022 amount.

None of this bodes well for Canada. When banks are stingy with credit, the rest of the economy feels it. There is a negative network effect: businesses can't grow, can't improve their productivity, can't hire more people, can't pay them more, and our living standards decline. Bank financing at current magnitudes is simply insufficient to finance the economic vitality necessary for Canada to have the robust and competitive economy we all covet.

Think of what the rate of small business growth might be if more credit were available on more reasonable terms. Canada, by any measure, is a rich country, but we lag behind the United States—a more dynamic economy—when it comes to our population-adjusted share of global GDP. Canada could be richer still if we could provide our entrepreneurs with financing. Instead, the early rewards of entrepreneurial risk-taking often go to the banks through high interest charges, and the risk of failure is left almost entirely borne by the entrepreneur.

Part One

Starting a business is one thing, but keeping it going over the years is quite another. Ten years after their birth, about 50 percent of small businesses with a maximum of four employees are gone, and at the sixteen-year mark, 70 percent of them have failed. Did the firms fail because the banks would not fund them sufficiently or were the banks right not to offer them any credit because they judged them too weak to survive?

The answer is we don't know. It is difficult to trace business failure to credit availability. All we know is that businesses in the sector that want credit, and likely can support it, cannot get it. Not only does this prevent businesses from taking off, it raises the chance that a small business will become insolvent because it is illiquid.

Some of Canada's banks do have private equity-like funding arms that provide financing to higher-risk businesses, but the businesses they finance are usually well beyond proof-of-concept. The interest rate charged on the debt component of financing can be onerous here, too, mostly in the low teens. Moreover, the enterprise must hand over much of its enterprise equity value as collateral.

Whichever way you cut it, our banks are not really in the business of risk. Even when they grant credit to large businesses, they set their investment banking arms to work crafting deals to shift large company loans from their balance sheets to the market through securitization, distributing them to other investors and taking a no-risk fee. So, in the end, banks don't much like to lend money to small *or* large businesses. But if they can find a way to charge a fee, you can bet they are all over that.

How did we get into this mess? How did a banking system intended to serve and support consumers and businesses wind up preying on them when it isn't ignoring them?

Canada, with its six large banks, has one of the most concentrated banking systems in the world. This high degree of concentration means that Canada's financial system is one of the most stable in the world. But with more concentration and stability comes less competition.

In general, our economy relies on competition to prevent one producer or group of producers from exploiting the customer. In the absence of competition, large companies have a lot of power to make decisions in their own interest. That's the situation with our banks. They decide who gets financed and who doesn't, and they set the interest rates at which loans are given and deposits taken. That means the price of bank lending, borrowing, and other services is not set by the market, but by the banks themselves without fear of challenge.

The absence of real competition is a market failure, where benefits are fewer than they would otherwise be and prices higher. When markets fail—especially when they fail to protect consumers— we expect competition authorities, backed by the government of the day, to step in. Canadian banks are regulated for safety by the Office of the Superintendent of Financial Institutions (OSFI), while the Financial Consumer Agency of Canada (FCAC) is charged with protecting the rights and interests of consumers. OSFI has delivered stability, but the FCAC is toothless and has been unable to prevent Canadians from being overcharged across a range of banking services, or at least those they can access. Meanwhile, the Competition Bureau, responsible for ensuring that businesses operate in a fair and competitive manner, has been disempowered.

We shouldn't be surprised.

Fundamentally, our government has a political preference for financial institutions over consumers. Political leaders have built and protected a financial system that primarily serves the interests of our highly profitable banks and their shareholders at the expense of everyone else.

It's time for serious banking reform to create a financial system that primarily serves Canadians and their economy.

PART TWO

Let's start with the basics. Economics is about dividing up scarce resources among us and using them efficiently. Achieving economic efficiency demands a way to get money where it is needed most. Our financial system builds and maintains the pathways along which money, or capital, travels from those who have it to those who put it to good use. It also directs the flow of money through the broader economy—all the buying and selling we do—at a price.

Banks sit at the centre of the financial system, essential pieces of our public infrastructure, albeit ones that are owned and run privately. They take deposits from earners, savers, and investors, on which they pay interest. The banks then use those deposits to make loans, for which they charge higher rates of interest. The interest received on the loan pays the interest to the saver, covers the bank's operating costs, and yields the bank a profit. Usually, a fat profit. That makes the interest rate one of the most important prices in the economy.

A Canadian bank's net interest income, or the difference between what it pays you for your savings and what it makes on its loans, is its biggest business, accounting for 52 percent of total revenue. The other 48 percent of its revenue comes in the form of non-interest income: an amazing array of service fees and commissions, plus income from trading stocks, bonds, and other financial products.

Banks are very skilled at attracting deposits at lower rates and lending out those funds at higher rates. They have been in the business of borrowing and lending for a very long time. Before a bank makes a loan to any individual or business, it must decide who is willing and able to service and repay the loan. Banks are experts at separating good borrowers from bad borrowers to keep loan losses low. Your bank probably has a deeper understanding of your financial situation, your financial habits, your willingness to pay, and the risk you present than you do—an exploitable knowledge advantage called *information asymmetry*.

If you're too much of a risk, your loan application will be denied. If you're so fortunate as to be accepted, the bank will take a hard look at how much money you earn and how much wealth you have. These are crucial signals about your ability to carry a loan and the risk of loss the bank might face if you default, and they determine the rate of interest you will pay on your loan. In general, a borrower with low income, a volatile work history, and few assets to back a loan, will pay a higher rate of interest than a high-income borrower with a stable work history and abundant assets (although, as we'll see, this isn't always the case).

All this expertise in reading signals and assessing potential borrowers helps banks stay rich. It also puts them in the position of deciding whose businesses get financed, whose consumer loans get approved, and whose do not. They decide which factory gets built, who gets a mortgage to buy a home, and who gets to borrow to build a new business. Banks are crucial institutions in our economy: if they aren't working optimally, it's a safe bet that the economy isn't working optimally, either.

Loan decisions are at the heart of a bank's operations. They should be neither trivial nor arbitrary. It is essential for both the bank's well-being and the economy that these decisions are taken seriously. When the bank makes a loan, it does not lend its own money, but rather its depositors' money. The bank has an obligation to pay depositors whenever they want their money back, just as the borrower has an obligation to pay back a loan. Any break in the covenant of trust on either side would quickly demolish the banking system as a whole and the economy along with it.

Of course, lending decisions are not infallible. There are always loan losses, which are absorbed by the bank's annual earnings. If the losses are large enough, they have to be absorbed by the bank's capital. If a bank's capital falls far below a government-mandated level, the regulators will shut it down; it is an article of faith and commitment that depositors are always paid back in full. Those are among the many reasons why banks are risk averse.

It is also in the interest of the Canadian economy that banks make good choices about who to lend their depositors' money. If our standard of living is to be maintained and improved over time, we need factories to be built, new businesses to be funded, and homes to be bought. Banks help all of this happen, and the better they do their job, the stronger our economy.

Ideally, all of this activity should occur within a competitive banking system. Canada has a market economy, which runs on the understanding that more competition among individuals and businesses in the provision of goods and services leads to more efficient outcomes. High levels of competition and efficiency bring the highest quality goods and services at the lowest possible price and provide the highest wages. That's the theory, anyway.

It follows that a competitive banking system is the best way to organize the distribution of income and wealth, ensuring that no one individual or enterprise gains at the expense of another, or is favoured over another, or is undeservingly left out in the cold. In a competitive banking system, it is very difficult for one banker or one small group of banks to exploit or ignore the consumers and businesses that rely upon them. Another bank down the street is always there to offer better terms. Competition maintains a level playing field. It also helps prevent banks from becoming too risk averse and only lending money to back sure bets.

Unfortunately, competition in the Canadian financial services industry remains an aspiration rather than a fact. We are one of the most concentrated banking systems in the world, and with more concentration comes less competition and more power in the hands of banks to decide who gets financed and who doesn't. If SMBs are deemed too risky by the major banks, they'll have to look elsewhere for funding.

In the absence of true competition, any given bank is free to determine the interest rates at which loans are given and deposits taken, and the fees at which services are provided, without fear of being undercut by a rival. That's the major reason banking is expensive in Canada. Compared to other jurisdictions, we see lower interest rates on our savings, higher interest rates on our loans, and higher fees on the broad range of financial services delivered by our banks—everything from payroll deposits to wire transfers to currency exchange to investment services.

Our government knows that our banking sector is highly concentrated and lacking in free and fierce competition. For that reason, banks are regulated to ensure there is some accountability for their actions and the prices they charge, even if the latter is done half-heartedly, if at all.

Canadian banks are chartered by the federal government. A charter is essentially a license, or legal permission, to operate a bank. It's a privileged position because few charters are given out, and it comes with a set of rules. There is a regulatory framework designed to ensure that banks conduct their business to high standards and that they maintain capital and liquidity requirements that ensure their stability, thereby protecting the interests of their individual customers. The trade-off is that banks face reduced competition in exchange for submitting to oversight and maintaining high standards of behaviour.

The system of charters has its advantages. For instance, it enforces desired standards of solvency, liquidity, and risk management that tend to make our banks stable and trustworthy. The belief is that because our banks are large, well-capitalized, and bound by the same rules, our banking environment is safe.

Safety is not the only consideration, however. Our system of charters and regulations is also expected to deliver an efficient banking environment, providing quality services at reasonable prices. One might think that having a small number of large banks with enormous scale would result in lower-cost services for consumers compared to a system of smaller banks with reduced scale. But that's not what happens. As we have seen, and shall see over and again in subsequent chapters, charters and government regulation have not prevented Canadians from being overcharged for banking services, or denied them.

Canada's small group of very large banks so thoroughly dominates our market for financial services that it can manipulate prices, stifle innovation, and choke off or buy out competitive threats. In fact, our banks have sufficient power to make the gains to economies of scale from concentration flow in reverse: instead of consumers and the broader economy benefitting from a system of large, stable, and efficient banks, the gains flow to the banks themselves and their shareholders.

None of this would happen if our government had a strong competition policy and enforced it vigorously. Unfortunately, our political leaders like the fact that our banks are stable. They fetishize stability, as though it were the only value in a financial system. This focus reinforces the lack of competition in the banking market and allows all manner of market distortions at the expense of consumers. The political leaders seldom ask if an uncompetitive, risk-averse banking system is worth its egregious cost to bank customers, taxpayers, and the economy as a whole.

How do we know when our banking system has too little competition and too much stability? A key indicator of how far an organization drifts from competition is how casually it treats its customers. Think about the wait times you endure when you call your bank. The cyber voice will tell you how valuable your call is, before making you wait to be transferred to a call centre. But the value you represent to the bank is inversely proportional to the time you spend waiting. The more music you hear and the more sales pitches you endure, the fewer resources the bank has put at your disposal, and the more resources it has directed to its executives and shareholders.

A better measure of diminished competition in Canadian banking is profits. By almost any standard, our banks are hugely profitable. They have an ability to generate extraordinary returns, year after year, a performance reflected in their share prices. Over the past three decades, the six big banks have been lapping other companies on the Toronto Stock Exchange (TSX):

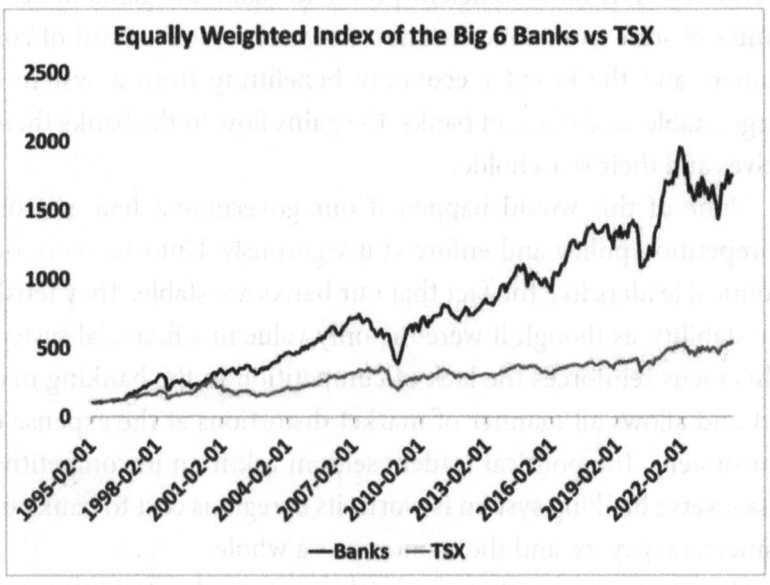

Even in the rarified world of large banks, Canada's entries stand out compared to the four largest US banks: Citibank, JP Morgan, Wells Fargo, and Bank of America. Their balance sheets look a lot like those of Canadian banks. They enjoy high degrees of market power and can extract high fees and pay lower deposit rates compared to smaller, regional US banks. Yet an index of the stock performance of the US big four ranks among the lowest compared to Canada's big banks since 2005.

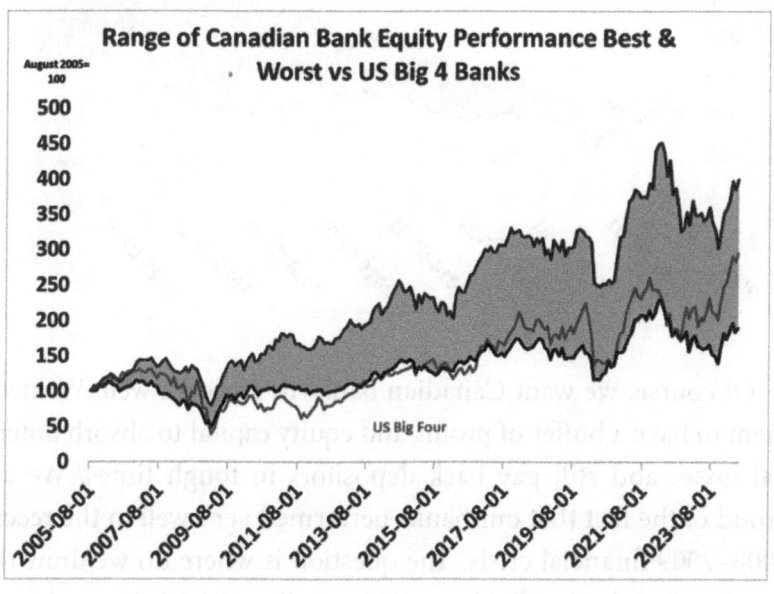

The United States has more than 100 regional banks; most of the smaller banks have more concentrated, less diversified lines of business, reflecting the less diversified local economies they serve. They are hypercompetitive, enjoying none of the dominance and price-setting ability enjoyed by either the Canadian or the large US banks. Here is their share price, measured by an index of regional bank performance as measured by the SPDR bank ETF over the last two decades, relative to Canadian banks.

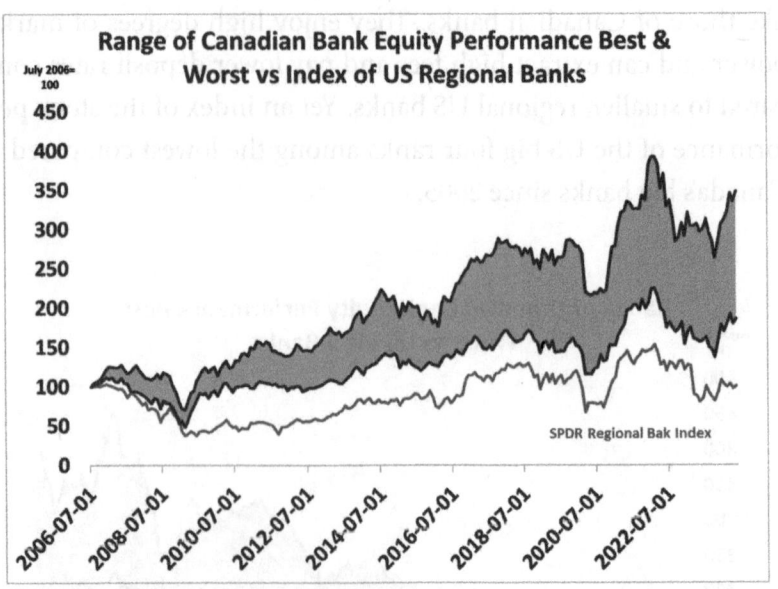

Of course, we want Canadian banks to perform well. We need them to have a buffer of profits and equity capital to absorb potential losses and still pay back depositors in tough times. We are proud of the fact that our banks performed very well in the recent 2008–2009 financial crisis. The question is where do we draw the line between letting banks perform well and letting people and businesses in the rest of the economy make a buck?

The cleanest read on the rate of return of any enterprise is what that enterprise earns after all of its costs have been met. For example, if the market value of a (small) bank's equity is $100 million and it makes $15 million in net profit every year, its return on equity is 15 percent.

Since 2008–2009, Canada's banks have on average generated a return on equity close to 15 percent, year in year out. If we dig deeper into the banks' annual reports and zoom in on their supplemental financial statements, we see a return on equity in their domestic (Canadian) personal and commercial businesses in the range of 22 percent to 42 percent across various banks and time periods. This is staggeringly large for a mature business far from the frontiers of discovery, innovation, and invention.

Conveniently, several Canadian banks, including TD and Bank of Montreal, engage in similar banking activity in the United States, allowing us to compare their return on equity in that more competitive market. For the financial years 2023 and 2022, TD's return on equity in its domestic personal and commercial business was 36.8 percent and 42.3 percent, respectively, compared to 14.2 percent and 14.0 percent in the United States. For BMO, the comparable returns were 26.6 percent and 38.6 percent at home and 8.8 percent and 17.4 percent in the United States.

What accounts for the difference in profitability between the two countries? Aside from elements of financial engineering, such as differences in the ratio of debt-to-equity financing, the gap in returns is mostly traceable to market share: Canadian banks dominate at home in a way they cannot in the more competitive US market. Their efficiency ratios, or their costs net of interest expenses, are significantly higher in the United States than they are at home because they don't have vigorous competition at home.

If you read about Canada's banks in the financial press, you'll often see their annual results and record profits presented by some as indicators of economic success. The banks are treated like other large corporations: their large profits are perceived as indications of a healthy economy and efficient businesses. But not all profits are alike.

Some firms make a lot of money by outperforming competitors and satisfying customers; others leverage a position of dominance to soak their customers while absorbing or otherwise taking out competitors. Profitability should never be assessed as an end in itself but rather as the reward for providing valuable products and efficient service.

Nor are profits a reliable indicator of broad economic health. They need to be judged in the context of other factors such as productivity and income growth. A business with high profitability may be signalling something less productive is at work, such as a reliance on suppressed wages and jacked-up prices.

Oxford University business professor Colin Mayer likes to divide corporate outcomes and success as a product of either solving or creating problems, as both can provide profit. Following this division, does Canada's financial system profit from solving or creating economic problems?

As we have seen, Canada's banks provide insufficient credit to entrepreneurs at high interest rates depriving the economy of dynamism. And as we will see, the banks charge shamefully high interest rates on credit cards, claiming a need to cover potential credit risk (default losses) that their own disclosures to buyers of credit card trusts demonstrate is minimal. They limit the terms and conditions of mortgages in their own favour. Their investment and wealth management operations charge fees so high that many savers lose almost half their lifetime savings to their banks, leaving them with insufficient capital to live well in retirement. These are clear examples of banks profiting from problems of their own making and a regulatory system failing to hold them to account.

PART THREE

Between 2002 and 2015, Ed Clark presided over TD Bank like a colossus, serving as its president and chief executive officer. In an exit interview with the CBC, he opined that the Canadian banking market was technically, but not behaviourally, an oligopoly. Reasonable people might disagree with Ed's assertion.

An oligopolistic market is one in which a few companies dominate the space sufficiently to extract above-normal market returns. It is similar to a monopoly, but the advantageous market position is enjoyed by a few firms, rather than one. It is fundamentally anti-competitive. Canada's banks unquestionably form an oligopoly.

Ed argued that to the extent Canada had a banking oligopoly, it was a good thing because it provided stability to the banking system. At the same time, he claimed that our banks compete vigorously within the oligopoly. In particular, he said, they fight each other to increase their share of the banking market. He argued that a shift of five basis points (five one-hundredths of a percent) is a big deal for a bank, demonstrating how what seems like a giant step to bankers might be imperceptible to mortals.

It is difficult to accept that the banking oligopoly husbands competition when, as we've seen, it clearly sustains profits well above competitive levels. Ed admitted in that same interview that investors in Canadian bank stocks have done well over the past few decades. He would like us to believe that this is a result of managerial skill. A better explanation is that the banks are exploiting the uncompetitive structure of their market.

The truth is that Canada's banking oligopoly wields great collective market power, enabling banks to set prices that transfer consumer income to their shareholders in ways other companies can only dream of. Yes, there is some rivalry among banks over market share, but this does not amount to genuine competition as most businesses experience it. The first rule of an oligopoly is to avoid intense competition that might spoil the party for the group as a whole.

Economists often cite the prisoner's dilemma when explaining the behaviour of oligopolists. In the prisoner's dilemma, two suspects commit a crime and get arrested. Police want to charge them both with the crime, but have insufficient evidence to secure a lengthy prison sentence for either of them. So the officers put the suspects in separate rooms and offer each a deal: rat on the other in return for more lenient treatment.

The police are hoping one suspect will turn on the other and they'll get at least one big conviction. That leaves each of the suspects with a dilemma. If the first suspect rats on his partner, he'll get a short sentence, and his partner will get a long sentence. But his partner is being offered the same deal. If she, too, rats on her partner, they'll both go to jail for a long time. If neither rats on the other, they'll both walk free. The key to resolving the prisoner's dilemma is for the suspects to agree before they commit the crime to keep mum.

Oligopolies behave in a similar way. If one company in the group cuts prices, it will steal business from the others, increasing its market share and profits; however, this will also force its competitors to follow suit and lower their prices. A price war ensues, and everyone loses. Best to have all members of the group keep prices at a comfortably high level so everyone earns a good profit. What the prisoner's dilemma tells us is that the gains from cooperation are greater than the narrow pursuit of an individual firm's interest.

It is no wonder, then, that there is no significant difference in the price of banking services in Canada, regardless of which bank you go to. Where there is a price discount in one service or product relative to rivals, it is often the case that another product or service is priced higher than at rival banks to compensate.

Ed Clark captured the challenges of the prisoner's dilemma—or, rather, the challenges of managing an oligopoly—in his interview. He was speaking about high housing prices. Credit supplied by banks has been bidding-up housing prices without inducing a positive housing supply response. By simply restraining their mortgage creation, banks could avoid a housing bubble and insulate themselves from the potential for big loan losses when it bursts. They would also help tame the price inflation that is threatening our broader economic and financial stability. Ed mentioned that while speaking to policy makers about how to cool the overheated housing market, he made them aware that if he pulled back from mortgage lending to deflate the bubble, one of the other banks would step in and fill his place. This he presented as competition. In fact, he was describing the behavioural dimension of life as an oligopolist and his inability to act independently.

CIBC's CEO Victor Dodig has also addressed the housing market, implicitly acknowledging the constraints on individual bank action. Instead of restraining his bank's mortgage lending to deal with steep home price increases, he has been advocating a policy that would see all levels of government work to increase the supply of houses to relieve price inflation in the real estate market. This is a sound argument if Canada wants to grow its housing stock. The recent surge in immigration has exceeded the ability of the economy's infrastructure to absorb people, suggesting that Dodig has a point. But what Dodig is really asking is that governments make the difficult decisions an oligopolistic banking sector cannot. Rather than manage their own risk, and potentially cede market share in mortgage lending to other members of the oligopoly, our bankers want the government to step in and rescue them from the jaws of the prisoner's dilemma.

That bank CEOs are averse to competition and are primarily concerned with maximizing the economic value of the group at the expense of the Canadian banking customer is not exactly a secret. It has been confirmed by researchers at the Bank of Canada, our central bank, or the banker to our banks. They found that the Canadian banking system is much closer to collusive oligopoly than perfect competition. Astonishingly, the Bank of Canada's researchers were untroubled by their findings, which is hard to square with the value economists generally assign to the benefits of competition.

As you might suspect by looking at their profit margins, the CEOs of Canada's banks take management of the oligopoly seriously. You could say they are experts in the art of oligopoly, which is more difficult and sophisticated a discipline than the raw exercise of market power.

For starters, it is illegal for the bankers to communicate with one another, even tacitly, on their business operations. Without ever discussing these matters around a table or in text messages late at night, they have to reconcile themselves to sharing the market. They must operate within the narrow band of acceptable business practices that have magically come to govern Canada's market for banking services, and trust that no one bank will strike out on its own to defy the reaction of others.

As they all row in the same direction and pursue mutually beneficial outcomes, the CEOs also must keep up the pretence of competition. They engage in lightly rivalrous activities, for instance,

Part Three

trying to poach another's customers now and then with advertising and special deals.

You can tell their hearts aren't in it—Canadian banks spend less on marketing and advertising than their counterparts in the United States, the United Kingdom, and Australia. But this minimum of jousting is sufficient to keep their market shares jumping around by five basis points each year, meeting Ed Clark's definition of competitive behaviour. Of course, it does nothing to interfere with mutually beneficial outcomes for the industry, and consumers continue to cough-up.

The proper management of an oligopoly also requires its members to maximize value without being too obvious about it. You can only raise prices so high, and squeeze so much economic value out of your business at the expense of consumers, before problems arise. Making customers squirm is fine; making them scream is counterproductive. They might revolt. New competitive threats might emerge. Regulators might turn up the heat.

To avoid these perils, banks are sophisticated in their maximization of fee revenue and loan prices and the minimization of deposit interest rates. While almost all of their prices are generally high, some are selectively pushed higher still through such tactics as price discrimination.

Price discrimination is the practice of charging different customers different prices for the same product or service. The coffee business does this with great skill. Starbucks charges $2.65 for a grande drip coffee and about $6.45 for a grande caramel frappuccino. What's the difference in the cost of producing each drink? Maybe 75 cents? A dollar? But certainly not $3.80. Starbucks isn't selling grande caramel frappuccinos for the enjoyment and satisfaction of its customers so much as to figure out which of its customers is insensitive to pricing.

Banks, too, are masters at price discrimination. Their trick is to exploit their information advantage. They know far more about your willingness to pay than you know about the real cost of a product or service. This can be as simple as giving new customers more attractive interest rates than those available to existing customers. The bank is counting on the existing customer finding it too troublesome to move to another bank with the same introductory offer (and banks do their best to make switching an administrative burden and a risk to one's access to credit).

Another way the banks practice price discrimination is by bundling products. For example, you can get a slightly better mortgage rate if you have your securities trading account at the same bank. As we'll see later, the wealth management business is a cash cow for the banks. You might feel like you're saving money on your mortgage, but you're leaking funds at a far faster rate in your investment account. This practice is widespread amongst the big Canadian banks.

The basic bank bundle includes an affordable chequing account, a savings account, and a credit card. The credit card is the key to determining a customer's price sensitivity. Credit cards come in many flavours, with a wide range of additional services, such as insurance, cash-back options, and travel credits that reach beyond the simple payment and loan functions of the card. Some create a sense of privilege for the card bearer—silver, gold, and platinum cards all printed on the same penny's worth of plastic. The banks, of course, would not be offering these benefits if they didn't improve profits by boosting revenues well above the additional service cost. Credit cards, as we'll also see later, are another cash cow, a means of pushing prices to new heights while providing the bank with valuable information on which of their clients is willing to accept a big mark-up over cost in return for a dubious boost to status.

Part Three

Yet another way to practice price discrimination is to leverage complexity. For most of us, the operations of banks are opaque. We have only a cursory understanding of how the financial world operates and we haven't the time, energy, or capacity to chase down the innumerable ways that banks are taking advantage of us. How, for instance, when we pay down our line of credit, the amount is deducted from your chequing account immediately but can take a day, or even up to five days, to show up as a payment to our credit balance. The bank holds our funds, pays us no interest for that privilege, and charges us extra days of interest on our outstanding credit balance. By delaying a day or five on millions of transactions over the course of a year, the banks substantially pad their profits. In the internet age, it beggars belief that this transaction is not completed instantaneously. The US Federal Reserve launched its Fed Now real-time settlement service for retail bank customers in July 2023. Canada's real-time settlement system, Real-Time Rail, has been plagued by delays and is unlikely to be operational until 2026, at the earliest.

Foreign exchange operations are another aspect of bank business beyond the grasp of most customers. Few of us follow the foreign exchange markets or pay close attention to the prices at which currencies are traded. We're unaware of the preferential rates at which banks and their institutional and corporate clients buy and sell currencies on the foreign exchange market compared to retail customers. Moreover, banks have no incentive to share this information with us, allowing them to charge us ridiculously high rates to buy and sell the foreign currencies we need for cross-border sales and receipts.

If the bank can buy a US dollar for $1.25 Canadian, it is likely to charge you $1.30 Canadian for that same US dollar, making five cents on every US dollar you buy. For a $1,000 foreign exchange transaction, the bank makes $50. On $100,000,000 of these transactions across its customer base, it makes $5 million. And so, bank shareholders profit hugely from the exploitation of the banker's information advantage and the lack of transparency in foreign exchange transactions.

These are just a few of the many cunning ways in which banks bolster their prices to meet their ever-escalating profit objectives. But, again, they can only push prices so far. The deterrent power of the regulator, plus fear of social opprobrium for obvious gouging, leads banks to choose a quiet life over conflict with society and its regulators. They don't want to wind up in the consumer affairs spotlight, as Loblaws has been in recent years, trying to justify healthy profits in a time of grocery price inflation. So banks rely on their other big lever for boosting profits at the expense of their customers: they squeeze from their business as much risk as they can.

We've already seen how banks have no interest in providing financing at a reasonable cost to SMBs, which they consider too risky. They much prefer to write low-risk mortgages that, for the most part, are fully collateralized by the property they fund, with any remaining risk underwritten by the government of Canada through the Canada Mortgage and Housing Corporation (CMHC). Finding the highest risk-adjusted returns—where returns are proportionately higher than the risk of loss—is the holy grail for bankers (and institutional investors, as well).

Even when they lend to established medium-sized businesses with revenues in excess of $10 million and solid credit ratings, banks do all they can to eliminate risk. The interest rates they'll charge can be onerous, mostly in the low teens. Once they write a loan, they set their investment banking arms to work crafting deals to shift it along with other large company loans from their balance sheets to the market through securitization. The loans then become another investor's risk and the bank takes a no-risk fee. CFIB consultant Mary Jane Grant was spot-on when she stated that "banks are not in the risk business."

Of course, it makes sense for banks to be sensitive to risk and protective of their businesses. The question is to what degree? A bank's purpose is not solely to reward its shareholders and its insiders through successful financial and economic engineering. Surely, as part of the financial system, banks have an obligation to facilitate economic growth. After all, banks are given their charters to facilitate the financial needs of both private and public sector activities. Banks are not chartered to be enterprises in their own right.

A good way to measure how little risk banks are taking relative to other parts of the economy, and how powerfully they funnel returns to their shareholders, is to look at the variability in the returns of bank stocks relative to the variability of the overall stock market. This is known as the individual stock's beta (economists, mathematicians, and financiers like to use Greek letters to define quantitative ideas). A beta of one indicates that a stock's price tends to move with the market. If the market increases or falls by 10 percent, the stock can be expected to rise or fall 10 percent. If the beta is above one, the stock moves by more than the market, displaying higher volatility and risk. And if the beta is less than one, the stock moves less than the market, displaying lower volatility and risk.

Canadian banks have a big weighting in the TSX, so if we compared bank stocks to the market, we would be comparing banks to themselves. To avoid this problem, we compare the banks to subsectors of the TSX that define a specific industry, such as IT and consumer staples. Relative to the TSX information technology subindex, the TD Bank, as just one example, has a beta of 0.45. Its beta compared to the subindex for consumer staples is lower still at 0.35. This means for a 10 percent move in the consumer staples subindex, the bank moves just 3.5 percent. This indicates that the bank's earnings are far less risky than those of other important industries.

Here's another way to look at it. Morningstar data from the second quarter of 2024 bank financial reports show that the cost of the industry's loan losses (gross impaired loan reserve) has risen to 0.79 percent. The average return on equity has also taken a downward dip to 12.3 percent in the quarter as the central bank keeps monetary policy tight (i.e., interest rates high) to combat inflation. Nevertheless, the ratio of return-on-equity to risk is a staggering high 15.5 to 1, even in an economic environment that is applying pressure to the banks' financial returns.

Canadian banking is a high-return, low-risk business by any standard. Instead of putting the revenue pedal to the metal—taking chances on loans to companies that might spark Canada's flagging productivity—the banks have slammed the risk brake to the floor. This approach helps bankers maintain that quiet life: they fatten themselves and their shareholders by reducing risk; the volatility of their stock prices is minimized; investors reward them with higher stock prices, relieving banks of the need to push service prices still higher.

Perversely, the quiet life is also preferred by the regulators who are supposed to be monitoring the banks on our behalf. The Office of the Superintendent of Financial Institutions, like most other government agencies, is staffed by bureaucrats, another risk-averse species. They want things to operate smoothly. They hate unpleasant surprises. It follows that they judge the banks' disproportionate focus on reducing risk to be innocuous, if not wise. Consumers might be getting a raw deal, but that's a problem for another government agency.

Part Three

The combination of increasingly expensive banking services and excessive risk reduction is hell on our economic prospects. Constrained credit creation contributes to our economic malaise by dampening the entrepreneurial flame. It is difficult to estimate what effect extreme risk reduction has had on economic growth, how many new businesses fail to get off the ground, and how many that do launch fail to grow for want of financing. But we do know that we aren't launching and growing enough small and medium businesses, and we know that the small-business sector represents the most dynamic half of our GDP and is collectively the largest employer in the country, accounting for two-thirds of jobs. Wage growth is driven by productivity, and the more capital—manufacturing machines, computers, information technology software, and training—each of us has to work with, the more productive we can be and the more we can be paid.

When small businesses can't access sufficient capital, productivity lags, and Canada's recent productivity record is pitiful. While all of Canada's economic ills cannot be laid at the feet of the banks, they are hugely complicit in our underperformance. Our banking system's obsession with risk reduction is a lead weight on growth in our living standards, which are further weighed down by very high service prices. The banks' business model is hindering our ability to both produce and consume, an outcome inconsistent with the privilege of their charters.

PART FOUR

The rate of interest levied on credit card balances borders on usurious and is perhaps the most egregious example of the banking system's exploitation of its information advantage it enjoys over its clients.

Credit card interest rates hover around 20 percent, roughly where they have been since the early 1980s when inflation and interest rates were in double digits. Canada's inflation has averaged about 2 percent between 1992 and 2022, and all interest rates have declined dramatically with it except credit card rates. Even as inflation has exceeded 2.0 percent for the past few years, the recent back-up in other interest rates remains well below credit card rates. In fact, one has to squint to see any decline in credit card interest rates since 1980.

Let's compare some numbers. In 1981, the interest rate on a Visa or a MasterCard was about 25 percent. Inflation was 12 percent, and the bank rate—the rate at which the Bank of Canada loans to the banking system—was a bit over 21 percent. The prime rate, or the rate of interest offered to a bank's best customers, was 22.75 percent, so the additional charge to use a credit card was a mere 2.25 percent, which compensated the bank for demanding fewer income and collateral requirements relative to prime loans.

In summer 2024, credit card interest rates are about 20 percent, with an even steeper 23 percent rate for a cash advance. The prime rate for the bank's best customers is 6.95 percent, putting the credit card spread at a whopping 13.05 percent. If you think that's disturbing, back in the pandemic years, inflation was 2 percent, the Bank of Canada's overnight rate was one quarter of one percent, and the prime rate was 2.45 percent. The credit card premium over the prime rate then was a staggering 17.45 percent compared to just 2.25 percent in 1981. The credit card interest rate has declined a mere 5 percent in forty years compared to a 20.3 percent decline in the prime rate marked in the depths of the pandemic, and 15.8 percent as of summer 2024.

Think about what an interest rate of 17.45 percent would do for your savings if you could get it. And bear in mind that your savings account was likely earning a fifth of one percent during the pandemic, and it's your savings that are contributing to the funding of the very credit card balance on which you pay about 20 percent.

Or compare that heavenly credit card investment return you can't get to the return on a government bond that you can get. If you were to invest $1,000 in a thirty-year Government of Canada bond at 3.3 percent, you would have $2,250 by 2053. Alternatively, if you were able to invest that $1,000 at 17.45 percent for thirty years, you'd have $124,621 by 2053.

The rates charged on credit cards are staggeringly rapacious, but many people are forced to pay them because they have no other borrowing options, at least none that come with the convenience of fewer income and collateral requirements.

The banks, in fact, prefer that you borrow against credit cards rather than take out a prime-based loan. To borrow at prime, the bank will ask for collateral, making the hurdle to a low(er)-rate line of credit more difficult to clear than the hurdle to credit cards. They do this because they make so much more money off credit cards.

OSFI data show that banks make almost as much every quarter on credit cards as they do on their entire mortgage book, which has a significantly higher principal value.

Pitifully, the credit card domain is where many small businesses have to go to access a small amount of credit. If you run a small business, the banks will give you a credit card with a $1,000 credit limit at an annual fee of $150. Say you use that card for payments and never run a balance. The $150 fee is equivalent to a 15 percent annual interest rate on a stand-by line of credit. And, if you need to run a balance to your limit of $1,000 for a year, the overall cost will be $350—the $150 fee plus 20 percent interest, or $200 in interest charges, on the amount borrowed. This gets you to 35 percent. If you happen to miss payments, the overall cost of the credit card climbs to about 40 percent.

Banks try to justify these rates by arguing that fraud is costly and that there is a relatively high "charge-off" or loss rate from card holders who default. They claim that only the least-reliable borrowers borrow at credit card rates. Yet banks are forever blitzing the public with mass mailings offering "low" rates to anyone who will sign up for a new or additional credit card. They are clearly hungry for more of this supposedly risky business. That suggests the returns of credit cards far outweigh the potential losses they incur for banks.

If only there were a way to determine the actual risk that credit cards represent for banks. Then we could weigh the merits of the banks' contention that credit card interest rates need to be sky high to cover the potential for defaults and losses.

Banks aren't stupid. They keep their default rates obscured so that they don't have to defend their borderline usurious rates of interest. As with every other instance of opacity in the banking world, it makes you wonder what they know that we don't know, and why they are reluctant to disclose key data. It's not even clear that bank losses from credit card defaults or fraud today are higher than they were in 1981 when the spread between credit card rates and the prime rate was much narrower. None of this information is disclosed, at least not directly.

Fortunately, the data on charge-offs is hiding in plain sight. You just have to know where to look for it.

We know that banks prefer fees to loans because a fee is booked today and there is no risk of loss in the future. It follows that banks bundle their credit card receivables into a security that is sold to investors. It's called a credit card trust. This shifts the risk of loss from the bank to the investor. When the banks do this, they must disclose all relevant details around the credit card trusts. For the sale to go smoothly, the trusts need a credit rating so that investors can price the risk they are asked to assume. This conveniently makes private information public for anyone who has the time to read and decode it.

According to Standard and Poor's 2020 ratings of credit card trusts issued by Canadian banks and retailers (Canadian Tire, for instance, has a credit card), the charge-off rate, or the default loss, is about 3.2 percent.

If this low charge-off rate for credit card loss as advertised to the investor community were widely known, there would be an uproar over the huge premium banks charge in such a low-risk business. The regulator, OSFI, certainly knows this information, and if our federal politicians had any interest in putting their constituents' interests first, they might fly the bank CEOs up to Ottawa and apply a little moral suasion on behalf of consumers. But our politicians have no appetite for such a conversation and CEOs are never obliged to change their ways.

There is worse information in the credit card trust filings. The banks advertise with pride to investors that the terms of credit card issuance are conservative, and that up to 32 percent of all credit card receivables are considered "super-prime," indicating a very low risk. These super-prime customers might want to ask their banks why they're not paying the prime rate of interest (which was around 2.45 percent at the time) rather than a credit card rate of 20 percent.

More outrageous still are the high rates of interest charged to a credit card borrower who slips up and misses a payment, as I once did during a busy period of life. After missing a monthly deadline, I received a message from TD Canada Trust—the people who advertise that their customer service is like sitting in a big comfy green chair—that screamed at me in capital letters like a text from Donald Trump:

THE LAST MINIMUM PAYMENT WAS NOT RECEIVED ON TIME. IF YOU MISS ANOTHER MINIMUM PAYMENT IN THE NEXT 11 CONSECUTIVE STATEMENT PERIODS YOU WILL LOSE ANY PROMOTIONAL RATE(S) AND THE ANNUAL INTEREST RATES ON THIS ACCOUNT WILL INCREASE TO 24.99% ON PURCHASES AND 27.99% ON CASH ADVANCES.

Contrary to its claim "that banking can be this comfortable," banking at TD Canada Trust can quickly become intimidating. The most interesting phrase in this bracing notice was "any promotional rate," aimed perhaps at new credit card recruits who could pose a worse credit risk than existing customers.

Even if one accepts the argument that missed payments are a precursor to default, it is ridiculous to charge a 5 percent increase in the lending rate on two missed payments. It borders on bullying. The banks, after all, are already charging a 13 percent spread over the prime rate, ostensibly to absorb losses.

Part Four

An obvious response to evidence of credit card gouging will be that credit card rates are no lower in the United States or other jurisdictions, and this is true. However, the United States and the United Kingdom are also highly concentrated markets. To justify one cartel's pricing by reference to another is like your child saying everyone in class got a D, so it's the teacher's fault.

What's the solution on credit cards? Apart from competition, transparency. We know that financial service fees are lower in countries with strong disclosure standards that emphasize transparency. Canada's banks fail on transparency. Canadian consumers are left in the dark, not knowing enough to cry foul and pressure politicians and regulators to act. That has to change.

PART FIVE

The biggest financial decision most Canadians will make is the purchase of a house. For most families, that house will be the primary way in which it builds wealth and winds up with something to pass on to future generations. Of course, homes are expensive, especially these days. Very few people can afford to pay cash for a place to live, so they turn to Canada's uncompetitive, bank-dominated, mortgage market to make a purchase.

A mortgage is a loan that provides you money to buy a house, with the house pledged as collateral to secure the loan. It gives the lender the ability to take your house should you fail to make regular repayments of the money borrowed, plus interest—lots of interest—perhaps as much, by the time you pay off the mortgage, as the amount you borrowed to buy the house in the first place. The rate of interest you pay is determined by the mortgage lender, usually your bank.

The mortgage rate has several components. Because the money the bank lends you to buy your house comes from funds deposited at the bank by savers, the chief component of the mortgage rate is how much the bank must pay those savers for their deposits. The bank adds something to compensate itself for administrative expenses, accepting the risk of a default on the mortgage, and the margin of profit that keeps its shareholders happy.

How do banks know how much to add to your mortgage to account for risk? Mortgage borrowers are a diverse lot. In an ideal world, the bank would charge each individual borrower an interest rate to reflect that individual's risk profile, but that would be a complex and expensive proposition. Instead, banks revert to rules of thumb to manage mortgage risk.

An important rule of thumb is the loan-to-value ratio. If the mortgagee makes an upfront investment, or down payment, equal to 25 percent of the value of the house, she borrows the other 75 percent of the purchase price. The purchaser's equity in the house is 25 percent and the loan-to-value ratio is 75 percent. The lower the loan-to-value ratio, the more comfortable the bank feels about the risk it is taking.

The down payment on a house is the new owner's "skin in the game." The lenders like higher down payments because housing prices sometimes fall. If you put 25 percent down on a house, a decline of 10 or 20 percent in the price of your house will wipe out a good chunk of your initial investment. You absorb the loss. The bank will be just fine. Mortgages are arranged so that the burden of risk lies mostly with the homeowner.

Banks like the homeowner's down payment to be big enough so that even if there is a major decline in house prices, the borrower still has some equity. If, in the aforementioned example, the house price drops more than 25 percent, a rare occurrence, the homeowner's initial investment is gone. She has negative equity and she'll be tempted to walk away from a house that now may be worth less than the amount of her mortgage. If she bolts, the bank will take over the property, hire a realtor, sell the property, and potentially absorb a loss. Banks are in the business of making loans, not in the business of real estate management.

The reality is that a very small number of borrowers default on their mortgages. The risk of default needs to be measured and managed by the banks, but in the absence of a major economic disruption, there are no mass defaults and, historically, mortgage losses have been small enough that banks can cover them with the excess of the mortgage interest rate over the deposit rate and still make a profit.

The challenge for many young aspiring homeowners is to save a big enough down payment for a house. This is especially difficult when house prices are rising much faster than income, as has been the case in recent years. Saving for the down payment has always been a challenge for young people, but today it has become next to impossible. A large portion of the population is locked out of the housing market. Even if young people are fortunate enough to raise a down payment, often their earnings are too low or too insecure to handle the ensuing mortgage payments, boosted beyond reach by the sheer scale of the mortgage necessary to complete the sale.

The Canadian government has done quite a lot to help aspiring homeowners achieve their dreams. Ottawa believes that homeownership is an important form of wealth accumulation and that it should be achievable for all. To that end, it encourages the banks to lend to borrowers who might not otherwise qualify by insuring those mortgages against default through the CMHC. (The government also allows homeowners to sell their homes without paying capital gains taxes on the amount the home has appreciated in value since purchase. Often this reflects overall price inflation, so it is a rare example of the government not applying an inflation tax.)

In business since just after World War II, the CMHC program remains a crucial mechanism for widespread homeownership. As we've seen, banks are enormously risk averse. Left to their own devices, they'd want all mortgage applicants to have at least a 25 percent down payment on their homes. Before World War II, down payments of 50 percent or more were typically required. Banks were treating mortgage applicants much as they treat today's small business owners seeking loans: only the best financed and most credit-worthy of applicants had any chance of success. As a result, rates of homeownership in Canada were low and the costs of mortgages were high.

In a sense, then, the CMHC insurance program was a response to market failure. The mortgage market was failing to supply sufficient mortgages relative to demand at the prevailing price. Once CMHC began insuring mortgages and protecting the banks from downside risk, the mortgage credit market was unlocked. With the government signing on to pick up the pieces when a mortgage went bad, banks were willing to accept higher loan-to-value ratios and far more families were able to purchase a house. Today, banks will approve homebuyers with as little as 5 percent down with the CMHC insurance backstop.

Canada's mortgage market is now enormous. According to the CMHC spring 2024 survey, the value of outstanding mortgages is about $2.16 trillion. Canada's banks are the big players in that market, claiming $1.6 trillion of mortgages outstanding giving them nearly 73 percent of the market. More than half of all mortgages in Canada are insured by the CMHC—insurance is mandatory in Canada if a potential borrower's loan-to-value ratio is above 80 percent.

Banks issue significant numbers of uninsured mortgages, but the emergence of the CMHC turned mortgages into an excellent business for the banks. They get most of the returns from a burgeoning mortgage market while the government shoulders nearly all the risk. Moreover, mortgage borrowers, not the banks, pick up the cost of CMHC insurance premiums (adding to the cost of their mortgages). Borrowers do sometimes default, usually because of job loss or poor financial decisions or family breakdown. When that happens, the CMHC compensates the lender. The bank foregoes interest payments after the date of default and must dispose of the abandoned property, but it's still a sweet deal.

So sweet that the banks would like to have it all to themselves. They have been working to tighten their stranglehold on this market. Forty years ago, trust companies were significant competitors for banks in the mortgage business. They, too, could take deposits and issue guaranteed investment certificates, or GICs, to fund their mortgage lending. The trust companies had a slight advantage over the banks in that they did not have to hold relatively costly central bank reserves against their deposits. The trust companies also offered advisory and management services that were denied to the banks, as the trust companies acted as estate trustees and pension plan administrators. Then federal policy changed in favour of the banks.

In 1991, Canada passed a revision to the Bank Act, reorganizing the Canadian financial system to allow banks to offer services that previously had been denied to them. A year later, Royal Bank of Canada acquired the failing Royal Trust Company. This was a classic example of a weak financial institution finding shelter in a strong institution. Mergers in times of financial difficulty and crisis are politically expedient, as they keep the state out of financial restructuring and protect taxpayers from having to cover the costs of a potential "bailout."

What is good politics is not necessarily good economic policy. Shotgun marriages between strong and weak financial enterprises are usually bad for competition. As the 1990s rolled into the 2000s, slowly but surely, the other banks absorbed many of the remaining trust companies to further dilute competition. The net result was a reduction in price competition in the mortgage market and a reduction in the availability of mortgages.

Crucially, the digestion of the trust companies by banks resulted in fewer branch offices throughout the country, which was central to the reduction in price competition. The physical presence of branches of different providers near to one another has been an important factor in sustaining competitive mortgage rate pricing. Once the banks absorbed the trust companies, they began to reduce their total number of branches for greater cost efficiencies, eliminating competition at the same time.

All was not lost, as competition emerged from new players. Non-bank mortgage lenders entered the market to blunt the worst of the impact of lost competition between banks and trust companies. Without the non-bank players, the competitive deterioration would have been significant.

The names of early non-bank providers include the Mortgage Company of Canada, Home Trust Company, and FirstLine Trust (insurance companies used to offer long dated mortgages at fixed terms, but these turned unprofitable as interest rates rose in the late 1960s and beyond). Unable to fund their mortgages through bank deposits and GICs, as did the banks and trust companies, these entities instead received equity financing to build a mortgage securitization business. They cut mortgages, bundle them into a bond, and sell the bonds to investors. The proceeds of the bond sales are then used to grant new mortgages, after which the process is repeated.

These new institutions avoided the infrastructure costs associated with opening branches and gathering deposits, and thus could offer a degree of price competition. Operating over the phone or online, they introduced personalized and timely service to the mortgage market, saving applicants the time and pain of going into a bank just to apply for a mortgage. They also shortened the time lag between mortgage application and approval from two weeks or more to mere hours.

At the same time, mortgage brokers emerged in the Canadian market, operating as intermediaries between borrowers and lenders. They lent their expertise to prospective homebuyers, helping them source and negotiate the best terms for their needs.

Initially, the banks saw the emergence of mortgage brokers as nothing more than another distribution channel that would help them to both maintain market share and reduce distribution overhead. But the brokers were quick to embrace the new alternatives to bank financing of mortgages. A whole infrastructure of independent lenders, brokers, and mortgage service companies suddenly began giving the banks a real run for their money. For a brief, shining moment, there was real competition in the mortgage market. The industry was suddenly more focused on servicing borrower needs than filling bank coffers. The alternative lenders managed to drive the banks' market share down from about 75 percent of all mortgages in the early 1990s to about 60 percent by the mid-2000s. It was a big deal, and a welcome one.

By this time, however, two ominous trends were emerging. First, the banks, following their usual playbook, began buying up the new competition to fend off the threat to a profitable line of business. CIBC kicked things off by acquiring FirstLine Trust in 1996. Also, the securitization of mortgages grew increasingly complex and risky, especially in the United States, which had seen a boom in subprime mortgages. These high-risk loans played a central role in the Great Recession of 2008–2009 and tainted the practice of mortgage securitization generally.

Canada was caught in the slipstream of the international financial meltdown. Our Great Recession was not driven by the securitization of weak mortgage or subprime lending as in the United States. Even though the chartered banks had joined independent mortgage lenders in the practice of mortgage securitization by 2008, with the blessing of CMHC, their participation was small in scale.

Canada's stability-obsessed regulators responded to the crisis by cracking down on the financial industry and securitization in particular, bringing innovation and competition in the mortgage market to a crashing halt. Given the distress evident in the US and the UK financial systems, there was little opposition.

In the post 2008-2009 crisis years, non-bank lenders retreated as a force in Canada's mortgage market, leaving only a few survivors such as MCAP. Some of the service improvements that had been forced by competition survived, but the pace of progress, innovation, and change slowed to a crawl. The so-called "non-regulated entities" such as Mortgage Company of Canada and Home Trust faced new limits on their ability to raise funds, stricter lending standards, and higher costs. They continue to offer mortgages, but in smaller volumes. Their footprint is much smaller, now just 10 percent of all mortgages granted.

All of this turned out quite well for the banks, which are back in a position of overwhelming dominance in the mortgage market. As of 2020, they have been funding two-thirds of their mortgages from retail and corporate deposits. The rest of the funding is raised in the market for securitized mortgages. All the mortgages in the securitized pool are insured by CMHC, which reduces the risk of loss for buyers of these instruments, helping the banks reduce the amount of expensive capital they need to hold by pushing mortgages off the balance sheet.

Best of all for the banks, they face little competition in this line of business. Like a true oligopoly, the individual banks each offer to potential borrowers very similar terms for mortgages—terms that maximize profit and minimize risk. One bank or another occasionally wants to grow its book and might offer better rates for a while, but this is time inconsistent and not strictly a measure of competition.

* * *

In the United Kingdom, amortization terms—the time allowed a homeowner to pay off a mortgage—of ten to forty years are available to homebuyers, with a twenty-five-year term being quite common. In the United States, lenders offer amortization terms of fifteen and thirty years with affordable fixed rates of interest throughout the term. This allows the borrower to lock in at a reasonable, predictable rate for the long run and avoid the potential shocks of sharp interest rate increases down the road. Similar options are available in some European companies. The value to consumers is immense.

Canadians have long been denied these options, even though many borrowers would undoubtedly appreciate the opportunity of lowering payments by stretching a mortgage out over thirty or forty years, and the security of locking in at a reasonable interest rate for the life of the mortgage.

The maximum term of amortization for an insured borrower in Canada is typically twenty-five years (recently stretched to thirty in very limited cases). And banks do their best to ensure that no homebuyers lock in interest rates for more than five years. There's always a chance that interest rates might rise over the long term to levels beyond which the banks have become accustomed to lending. They don't want to be caught with mortgages at lower rates than they need to pay savers. While there is not much risk in the Canadian mortgage sector today, given the presence of CMHC insurance, any risk is seemingly too much for our conservative banks. They could mitigate their risk through hedging, but they prefer instead to limit fixed-rate mortgages to five years or less. While ten-year fixed-rate mortgages are available, they are disadvantageously priced to keep demand low. This leaves homeowners at risk of refinancing multiple times with unpredictable rates of interest over the life of a mortgage. It's unfair, but it's not in the banks' interest to offer better terms. There is insufficient competition to force their hands. And governments haven't the fortitude to demand change.

Part Five

Some entrepreneurs have attempted to compete with banks, aspiring to provide long-term mortgage solutions, financing them through securitization. But our various federal housing agencies have not supported long-dated, securitized, mortgage innovation. If they had, consumers might have welcomed the option of enhancing their household financial security and personal financial stability with these alternatives, even if they were a bit more expensive than shorter term mortgages. Innovation might also have reduced the overall interest-rate risk faced by households and helped stabilize Canada's overheated and over-indebted housing market. Instead, the innovators were snuffed out for fear that they would boost demand for housing and drive prices higher (that horse had already bolted). As usual, the government put stability ahead of innovation. The end result has been to leave households in the cross-hairs of market risk, undermining personal financial security.

PART SIX

There are a number of ways Canadians can grow their wealth. They can use their savings to buy a home or start a business. They can leave their money in a savings account and earn a miserably low rate of interest. Or they can do what about 40 percent of Canadians do: invest in capital markets by buying stocks or bonds, usually through the wealth management department of their bank.

If you are interested in wealth management, your bank will set you up with an investment adviser. Investment advisers come with different names and different price ranges, but what matters is that they offer services for a flat fee based on the value of the assets you give them to manage, somewhere in the range of 1.0 percent to 1.5 percent, each and every year. As your assets grow, so does the dollar value of the fee extracted by the bank. You can see why the wealth management business is so attractive to banks.

Ostensibly, clients pay wealth management fees to get access to expert investment advice, which might range from financial planning to asset allocation, to investment manager selection. One adviser may offer stock-picking advice by leveraging research from the investment bank's analysts. The pitch is that the adviser will help you "beat the market." Most will direct you to mutual funds— collections of stocks, bonds, or other securities selected by well-paid mutual fund managers to save you the trouble of learning how to pick your own stocks. There are thousands of mutual funds available, and for reasons that will soon become apparent, your adviser will likely direct you to mutual funds owned and managed by the bank itself.

Let's look at a common type of mutual fund arrangement for plain vanilla equity and fixed income funds. You, the investor, walk into the branch, deposit some funds, and get hooked up with the wealth manager to whom you'll pay that commission of about 1 percent on your investments for as long as your relationship lasts, regardless of how much wealth you accumulate. If you have a good run, those fees may drop to keep you in the tent, but good runs are hard to come by when the first 1 percent of gains go to the bank. The wealth manager is likely to recommend you put your money in one of the bank's mutual funds, files the paperwork, and that's it. Apart from that modicum of self-interested advice, you might get a phone call from your wealth manager once a year.

The mutual fund in which you are now invested also levies its own fee, in addition to that charged by the bank. In most cases, roughly 1.5 percent of the money you have invested goes to a mutual fund manager, every year. This is to cover the costs of managing the fund and compensates the fund manager for his or her expertise.

Adding up these fees, including any additional fees your adviser might be paid either up front or at the end of your investment (trailing fees), you may end up paying a combined fee of 3 percent split between the bank for advice plus a management fee to the fund manager each year for the privilege of owning a typical mutual fund.

If you are fortunate enough to have $1 million to invest facing a fee of 3 percent, that comes to $30,000 a year. You only begin to get paid once that $30,000 per annum is covered. In other words, the mutual fund in which you're invested must grow by more than 3 percent every year simply to keep your wealth from diminishing.

What is the value of the advice you get from your wealth manager and the expertise applied by your mutual fund manager? On the whole, given the costs, not much. The only way you'll get value for your money is if your adviser directs you to a mutual fund whose manager is consistently achieving above-average gains or below-average losses. That means better returns than you'd get by randomly selecting stocks from the TSX or NYSE or the S&P 500 or the NASDAQ, or better returns than you'd get by spreading your money across all available stocks on those markets.

Much of the mutual fund industry is based on the notion of "star managers," Oz-like figures who supposedly have great aptitude for picking the best-performing stocks for inclusion in their funds. (The returns of a given stock come from the company's dividends, plus the rate that its earnings grow, plus or minus the change in price that the market will pay to own a piece of the company, reflecting confidence in its future cash flows.) However, the consensus from decades of research is that most mutual fund managers do not consistently outperform a random selection of stocks, especially after accounting for fees and expenses. Moreover, many studies have shown that mutual fund managers usually underperform the market (the whole index of investable stocks), especially after accounting for fees and expenses.

If you are fortunate enough to see your mutual fund investment jump 20 percent in a year, it's likely because the broader market has experienced a banner year, not because your mutual fund manager is brilliant. Nor do many mutual fund managers do a better job of managing the downside—avoiding those devastating slumps in the value of your holdings that makes wealth accumulation a white-knuckle sport.

Even some of Bay Street's best-known fund managers seriously underperform the market. Their performance records are often buried in disclosure documents. Drawdowns, a measure how far a fund falls from its most recent high, and how long it takes to recover from its new low to the old high, are rarely shown. One celebrated "star manager" whose ego exceeds his long-term returns has taken years to recover the value of his fund from the high-water mark before its fall. Instead, the fund's disclosure documents trumpet recent short-term returns the manager has achieved so obscuring underperformance.

The smart money, to the extent it uses mutual funds, avoids these "stars" and instead looks for systematic fund managers who follow a scientific method. Some mutual fund providers do demonstrate sustained skill, beat the market, and earn their fees, but they are exceedingly rare. Other fund providers offer financial engineering skills to deliver relatively high yields each year and maximize the value of compounding by avoiding large market drawdowns. The performance across these mutual and ETF fund vehicles varies, but there is some skill for sale. Whether these providers can challenge bank dominance of the industry remains an open question.

There is a better way for most consumers to invest their wealth in capital markets. Exchange traded funds (ETFs) are an alternative to mutual funds, one that is mostly passively managed. Essentially, ETFs allow you to buy-and-hold the whole of a given asset market rather than pick-and-choose individual stocks you hope will outperform. This offers you a market-based return, which is almost always as good as or better than the mutual funds your bank will recommend. Better still, ETFs have very low management fees; being mostly passive investment vehicles, there is nothing to manage other than the costs of supporting the market infrastructure. They cost about a tenth (or less) of management fees at competing mutual funds, and less still if acquired through a direct-investing channel.

Larry Bates' excellent book, *Beat the Bank*, offers this astonishing example of how much mutual funds eat into your wealth compared to ETFs. Imagine that your parents invested $100 for you when you were five, and that the annual return was 6 percent for the next fifty years. Now imagine that you're receiving a 6 percent return in a mutual fund recommended to you by your bank. The management fee is 2 percent per year. So instead of receiving 6 percent every year, you receive 4 percent, which drastically reduces your ability to benefit from compounding. At the end of fifty years, the value of your portfolio is $710 instead of the $1,842 you would have realized at the full 6 percent.

By taking 2 percent of your asset value every year, the bank destroyed $1,132 of your potential growth, and earned $269 in management fees—a third of your gains—in return for its terrible, self-interested advice. Had you put the same $100 in an ETF with a 0.2 percent management fee, your initial investment would have been worth $1,676 after fifty years. The ETF would have cost you a mere $166.

ETFs and their cousins, index funds, are rare examples of competition in the financial system that makes the banks feel the pinch. They are an American innovation, pioneered by Jack Bogle, founder of The Vanguard Group. Something of a traitor to the traditional mutual fund industry in which he started his career, Bogle, knew that most investors, including many professional fund managers, can't forecast the price swings on individual stocks, and that actively managed mutual funds tend to deliver underwhelming returns, especially after fees. He realized that it was better for most people to just buy a piece of the entire market, sit back, and ride out the ups and downs. Index funds, introduced by Bogle in the 1970s, are a cheap and easy way to do this.

Index funds and ETFs didn't begin to make their way to Canada's conservative financial system until the 1990s. Despite the wide availability of these cheaper and better performing alternatives, a majority of Canadians were still holding mutual funds in their Registered Retirement Savings Plans (RRSPs) as late as 2018. ETFs and index funds are gaining ground, but many Canadian investors, at the urging of their banks, continue to pay high fees for plain vanilla mutual fund that require no real management skill and deliver mediocre returns. In fact, Canadians have about $2 trillion spread over thousands of mutual funds, the vast majority of the actively managed, high-fee variety.

Morningstar, a financial services research company, conducts a biannual assessment of value for money in the global mutual fund industry. The most recent assessment available is 2022. They find that Canada is just about the most expensive place in the world to own a mutual fund.

Why does Canada continue to get such poor grades in the Morningstar studies? Because we have a closed mutual fund market that puts investors at the mercy of the domestic financial services industry, and particularly our banks.

Morningstar finds that investors benefit when there is transparency about the costs of mutual funds, and fund managers benefit when there is a lack of transparency. Its analysis shows that in countries with robust regulators that demand full disclosure of mutual fund fees, those fees tend to be a lot cheaper than in places with obscure and complicated fee opacity, like Canada.

This is another instance of banks taking advantage of their enormous information advantage over customers. Levying fees, again, is the biggest, easiest part of their business. It's far easier to take 1 percent of an investor's capital every year for advice, and a share of the 2 percent as a mutual fund fee, than it is to develop the skills and tools required to regularly beat the market. Best, then, for the banks to deploy their resources on investment advisers and marketing that steers customers into high-fee investment vehicles.

The information advantage enjoyed by banks could be levelled by true transparency, but that would require firm regulation. Canada is distinguished by the persistence of a clubby relationship between the financial industry and the politicians and regulators. Instead of paving the way for more consumer-friendly investment vehicles, the politicians and regulators are more inclined to shield the Canadian mutual fund business from global competition.

Most ETFs are provided by offshore entities. Their best access to the Canadian market is through our chartered banks, where most Canadians do their investing. They have to endure extended periods of performance review and due diligence inspection before they can tap into these valuable channels. This has a chilling effect on new entrants and innovation in the industry. Banks have no incentive to make the processes any easier. They want to continue to recommend their own mutual funds to their clients, keeping all the fees in house rather than seeing assets flow out to an independent mutual fund.

Another problem with our system of securities regulation is that it is balkanized by province, and every province wants to run its own show, expand its powers, and resist centralization. As a result, the individual provinces cannot agree on common disclosure standards for mutual fund fees. Lobbyists for the industry are expert at exploiting these differences. They have been especially effective in Ontario, where the Ontario Securities Commission, under intense pressure from Bay Street, has delayed much-needed reform.

Some progress is being made. The banks have responded to this rare bit of competition and are now reluctantly making available low-cost ETFs. A number of independent managers—aspiring John Bogles—have introduced innovative products and carved space

Part Six

for themselves in the Canadian industry. And while Morningstar's 2022 rating for Canada's fees and expenses was still below average, it acknowledged that transparency in fee and access disclosure has improved. Many retail investors nevertheless remain locked into expensive mutual funds both manufactured and sold by their banks.

* * *

Another investment innovation that was slow to cross the forty-ninth parallel is the discount brokerage, or the customer-direct investing model. Banks offer discount brokerage services that allow you to buy and sell stocks, bonds, and funds on your own, without the benefit (and fees) of a wealth manager. If you chose direct investing, the bank will not give you any advice. In fact, it's prohibited from doing so.

Obviously, discount brokerages are a bummer for the banks. They lose the wealth management fees, and it's more difficult for them to direct their customers to bank-owned, high-fee mutual funds. To redress this setback, they encourage trading and charge high fees for the buying and selling of stocks. Canadians pay $9.99 a transaction for market access that the bank can accomplish for pennies.

It seems that banks have also been able to hang on to some of their fee revenues even though they are prohibited in providing advice in their discount brokerages. In its 2021 audit of the Ontario Securities Commission, Ontario's Auditor General found that discount brokers were receiving commissions from mutual fund companies whose funds were purchased by direct DIY investors. Up to $400 million was raked in by discount brokers between 2016 and 2019 for advice they couldn't and didn't give. If this wasn't a scandal, what is? A class action suit is now underway to recover the fees, and in 2022 discount brokerages were banned from collecting such commissions.

The Auditor General's report had a lot more to say about the mutual fund industry, particularly its egregious fees: how investors pay fees to everyone along the mutual fund industry chain; how they keep on paying as long as they are invested in mutual funds and in ever-increasing dollar amounts; how the fees and commissions paid by mutual fund companies to advisers to direct your savings to them come not as an expense to the mutual fund company but as a charge to you; how you must pay those fees even when the adviser and the mutual fund are housed in the same bank, and so on.

The Auditor General estimates that the commissions paid by the mutual fund industry to advisers—and ultimately picked up by investors—cost almost $14 billion in the province of Ontario between the years of 2016 and 2020.

The securities regulators of both the United Kingdom and Australia banned these embedded commissions in 2012. Both jurisdictions require the financial industry to work to a fiduciary duty, which puts investor interests first and prohibits many of the Canadian industry's most lucrative practices. It ensures fee transparency and, even more importantly, investors only pay once, not annually, and at an ever-increasing rate. They get to keep the bulk of their capital gains rather than passing them through to their advisers and the sponsoring banks.

The mutual fund industry has such a powerful lobby in Ontario that most bank-enriching, investor-soaking commissions remain alive today. The industry continues to pressure the Ontario Securities Commission to keep the party going for as long as possible. It advocates for what it calls "client-focused reforms" over fiduciary duty. Client-focused reforms lack the higher legal obligations of fiduciary duty and allow advisers to continue to earn higher commissions by steering investors' savings to the highest commissions on offer by the mutual fund industry. While advisers and their parent companies in Ontario are required to have systems in place to manage a conflict of interest, they are mostly ineffective, leaving it up to the adviser and dealer company to act if a conflict is flagged. The agent that creates the conflict is given the discretion to manage it.

Industry lobbying is a significant reason why the pace of rule change in Ontario is "extremely slow," notes the Auditor General. The cozy relationship between the mutual fund industry and its regulators at the OSC is apparent in the latter's 2021–22 statement of priorities. Investor protection is not even mentioned in the regulator's "top-level" goals. Rather, the emphasis is on promoting confidence in Ontario's capital markets by reducing regulation, facilitating financial innovation (the motivation for which is often to skirt regulatory constraints), and a vague commitment to strengthening the organization's foundation.

When the Attorney General investigated reasons for the OSC's industry-focused mission, issues of governance and the selection of OSC commissioners bubbled to the surface. Commissioners are mostly chosen from the ranks of former industry executives—in other words, people who long ago learned how to put the interests of shareholders ahead of corporate and public purpose. Rare among OSC commissioners is a true advocate of investor interest. The fox is well and truly in charge of the hen house as it is across many of Canada's board rooms.

What's still more aggravating is that banks have an entirely different set of rules when dealing with customers who can best afford to pay large fees and commissions. Institutional investors—pension funds, insurance companies, independent investment banks, and hedge funds—are able to negotiate the terms on which they deal with banks. They have a degree of sophistication equal to that of the banks' most skilled financial engineers, and they can direct significant pieces of business to the banks. So both sides work together to solve financial problems. The banks have an incentive to keep these big clients coming back; they treat them respectfully. Not so our poor retail client.

There are ways that the mutual fund industry could give individual investors some of the respect they show for institutional clients, although they would end the party for the industry and the banks. All those commissions that do real harm to an investor's wealth-building aspirations are indefensible. There needs to be a clear link between benefits received and fees charged so that investors can determine whether they are receiving value for money. Full transparency on fees and their cost to investors is essential so that investors can make the best choice to better balance risk, reward, and cost. Full disclosure on commissions paid leads to better-informed investors and accountable providers. Such transparency, championed by a requirement for "fiduciary duty" rather than "client-focused reforms" would bring more alignment between banks, the mutual fund industry, and investor interest.

Competition is always the best antidote. The introduction of low-fee ETFs has already forced some lowering of fees on mutual funds. And banks' habit of using their gatekeeper status to keep more efficient and innovative third-party providers of investment funds off their distribution platforms is increasingly being challenged.

Transparency and regulation still have a long way to go for the full benefits of institutional investor skill to make it to retail clients at a reasonable price. In the meantime, millions of Canadians remain captive to a bank-led investment environment that can only be described as collective self-harm.

PART SEVEN

How did Canada end up with so few banks, and so few alternative outlets for financial services? The answer is a long, serial history of bank creation and failure, with the weak chased into the arms of the strong, and a blithe acceptance of oligopoly by politicians dodging blame for inadequate regulatory policy.

Canada's first bank was an offshoot of the First Bank of the United States, which received its inaugural charter from the new republic, granted by Alexander Hamilton, in 1791. The Canada Banking Company was founded in 1792 in Montreal. It went nowhere, like a lot of banks founded in the late eighteenth and early nineteenth centuries in the British colonies that would become Canada. They were small, regional banks, and few lasted even five years.

The first to demonstrate real momentum was the Bank of Montreal, founded in 1817, although its charter was not approved until 1822. It quickly sought to expand into Upper Canada (present-day Ontario) but was blocked by politicians' intent on protecting locally owned banks, a glaring sign of things to come.

Bank of Montreal finally elbowed its way into Upper Canada in 1838, purchasing the wobbling, Toronto-based Bank of the People, an early instance of consolidation in the sector, and another foreshadowing of things to come. At this point, however, mergers and acquisitions weren't altogether bad. The colonies' many small banks were mostly limited to small, undiversified, local economies. They had no protection from deep cyclical swings in those economies and the constant structural changes that affect any locality or region. Those able to merge with or acquire another bank gained a measure of diversification. Exposure to broader markets was an antidote to the high frequency of bank failure.

The many nineteenth-century bank collapses caused no end of local or regional distress and political troubles for the governments of the day. Various commissions into the causes of these failures shone a bright light on inadequate regulation and supervision. The net result was an early political preference for stability over competition, an inclination reinforced by the prevailing ethos of British colonial rule. We may be vexed by our obsession with stability today, but we came by it honestly.

The concern for stability also led to the imposition of high capital requirements for the banks. This was a development urged not only by politicians looking to avoid turmoil, but also by established bankers who preferred to limit competition.

Once the Canadian Bank of Commerce was founded in the year of confederation, 1867, Canada's big six banks were all in place (the Commerce would merge with the Imperial Bank of Canada in 1961 to make CIBC). Each is now more than 150 years old, whereas the average lifespan of a company on the Standard & Poor's 500 index is about twenty years. That's a ridiculous amount of stability.

The almost forty chartered banks in Canada in the 1880s were winnowed down to eight by the end of the World War I, of which five had national reach (National Bank then limited itself to Quebec), and not much has changed since. Upstart banks came and went. Trust companies, established in the nineteenth century and long able to offer competition to the banks for certain services, were eventually absorbed by the big six, either because of near failure or to satisfy bank hunger for growth and fatter profit margins. The surviving independent trust companies do little more than execute fiduciary duties as asset custodians and managers. They are not a viable alternative to the banks.

In the early twentieth century, and especially during the Great Depression, small cooperative lenders emerged to serve individuals and regional associations. They grew up into today's credit unions, which were seen by their founders as alternatives to the banks. These are deposit-taking and loan-granting institutions, just like banks, but they are regionally concentrated and fall mostly under provincial regulation. Some credit unions have gone national but must accept federal regulation to do so.

Credit unions are dwarfed by the big six and using balance sheet size as a crude measure of presence, the combined assets of the sector are roughly the same size as the smallest of the big five banks in the country. Not only are they smaller, but credit unions are organized differently than banks. Each branch relies on a central agency to provide treasury functions, leaving it to take in deposits and make loans to consumers and small businesses. They do not offer the full range of payments and cash management services that a bank does.

That brings us to Canada's payments system. The payments system is the critical piece of infrastructure, or plumbing, that allows money to flow to where it is needed among financial services companies, and to consumers and businesses. The banks control it. The payment system acts as both a castle wall and a moat for the banks, repelling twentieth and twenty-first-century competition.

This problem was recognized over forty years ago. The payments system was then run by the Canadian Bankers Association, the bank lobby group, and it controlled access to favour the banks. Dissatisfied with this anti-competitive structure, the federal government took responsibility away from the CBA and formed the Canadian Payments Association (CPA) as a non-profit entity in

1980, hoping it would level the playing field by allowing access to all who qualified.

It didn't. The banks continued to be the major shareholders in the CPA and managed to reassert their dominance over it. Smaller alternative players were denied direct access and had to travel through the banks to service their clients. Having failed to meet its founding mandate, the CPA was dissolved. Payments Canada rose to take its place in 2016.

Payments Canada was essentially a rebranding of CPA with a new governance regime and a mission to modernize Canada's payment infrastructure and support innovation in the payments ecosystem. The idea was that non-bank members would be welcomed in, aligning Canada with payment systems in the United Kingdom and Australia—jurisdictions that do not tolerate the sidelining of alternatives to the big banks. One of Payments Canada's signature initiatives was Real-Time Rail, which was supposed to enable instant payments and support a greater variety of person-to-person, business-to-business, and government payments.

Unfortunately, the new governance regime came up short and Payments Canada—you can't make this stuff up—handed over day-to-day management of the system to none other than Interac, the bank-owned network that facilitates customer electronic payments. Unsurprisingly, Real-Time Rail, the instantaneous payments and clearing system that promises to revolutionize payments system access, experiences serial delays. It is still in the process of being implemented and, at present, no new launch date has been specified.

Access to the payment system will theoretically allow all participants faster payment processing, providing non-core players with the ability to provide a greater range of services and a chance to better compete with the banks. The lack of progress with Real-Time Rail, however, has taken the shine off this opportunity, as have the onerous fees, technological infrastructure costs, and regulatory hurdles that accompanies access to the payment system.

Every time the federal government tries to end bank control of a payment system that stunts competition and innovation from non-bank entities, it has fallen short of its goals. Our government is the monkey in the mirror. A monkey fails to recognize its own reflection in the mirror and instead sees an aggressor and reacts defensively to its own movements. The monkey consigns itself to an endless feedback loop of activity with no resolution. This is consistent with the entire experience of federal regulation of the banking industry: All efforts to restore competition have resulted in the banks remaining in pole position.

* * *

If Canada cannot create home-grown competition for the banks, perhaps foreign banks can do the job for us? Many foreign banks dwarf Canada's banks in size and outpace them in the rate of technological advancement. Could they not shake up the industry?

Not really. The entrenchment of the Canadian banks in this market combined with Canadian capital and liquidity requirements, and the ability of these banks, if they so desired, to offer service levels equal to those of foreign banks, makes Canada a tall order for outsiders. Add to that Canada's geographic expanse and small population, and we aren't an especially attractive market. Any threat from foreign invaders, moreover, would prompt Canadian banks to beat the Maple Leaf drum and alarm the public and policy makers about threats to everything from jobs in the industry to the stability of our financial system.

Additionally, many of the large global banks in their domestic markets look an awful lot like Canadian banks. Given the enormous start-up costs that would come with entering the Canadian market, it is not clear that a big bank, on arrival, would want to provide meaningful price competition with our banks, or extend credits to borrowers our risk-averse banks have turned down. They'd be more likely to attempt to recover their start-up costs by imitating, as far as possible, the fat-margin behaviour Canadian banks evince.

Finally, it's not the right time. Global banks are retreating to core home markets. The HSBC decision to exit Canada can be traced to its pullback from universal global banking. The risks of going global were made painfully clear by the 2008–2009 global financial crisis. Banks that were international in life became national in death. It is not likely that any global bank will enter Canada to challenge domestic bank dominance soon, if at all.

If not foreign banks, what are the other options? While some of Canada's life insurance companies have small banks, banking is not their primary corporate purpose, and they, too, shy away from the huge cost barriers that make Canada's banking market uncompetitive.

More promising is fintech. Financial technology companies promise to deliver key banking services through the internet or an app, bypassing the brick-and-mortar banking system altogether. They also "unbundle" the bank, focusing on delivering one or two banking products really well rather than trying to match the full range of chartered bank services. As well, they tend to demonstrate an unaccustomed openness, giving customers the ability to own their data and readily move between providers.

Despite the high start-up costs involved, fintech attracted financing from angel investors, because it has a clear value proposition, providing discrete solutions for customer pain points created by conventional banking's relative indifference to customer service.

Part Seven

Canada has a fairly long list of fintechs that have achieved household recognition, such as non-bank wealth manager WealthSimple. But without full access to the payments system, WealthSimple is plagued by a settlement delay of three days as funds are transferred. That undermines its ability to capture new investors.

As an illustration of what is possible, the UK payments fintech Wise was connected to the Bank of England's Faster Payments System in 2018 (six years ago no less) and as a result has reduced access fees by 20 percent and processing times from fifteen minutes to less than twenty seconds. Wise is now a significant player in global payments, but has yet to be granted access to Payments Canada.

These few examples illustrate the full power of fintech to disrupt traditional banking and introduce a measure of badly missing competition. But they also demonstrate the ability of banks to thwart innovation through their stranglehold on access to the payments system. The banks are aided in these efforts by our government's ponderously slow introduction of enabling legislation for reform of the financial system.

There are other threats to fintech's promise, including the possibility that their methods are co-opted by banks to serve their existing business models and capture higher returns for their shareholders. And to the extent that fintech companies succeed, banks could do what they've always done in the past—acquire them to eliminate a competitive threat or to gain advanced systems to overcome years of underinvestment in their own technological backbones.

The fate of Dutch bank ING's operations in Canada is instructive. Branded ING Direct, it provided non-branch access to banking services via the internet starting in 1997. With a link to the payments system through an existing account at one of the big banks, ING offered no-fee banking and attractive interest rates on deposits and loans.

It was a positive, disruptive force in the Canadian banking environment. However, instead of living up to its competitive promise, ING Direct was acquired by Scotiabank in 2012 and was rebranded as Tangerine. Scotia needed to broaden access to domestic deposits that its branch system could not reach, and it wanted ING's digital network to overcome its prior underinvestment in technology.

Another promising banking development related to fintech is open banking, which was pioneered in the United Kingdom. In 2016, the UK Competition and Markets Authority instructed nine of its big banks to open their customer data both to consumers and to third-party service providers. The reforms were enacted by 2018. They gave individuals more transparency and control over their finances and the ability to use different products and services across financial institutions while making it much easier to leave one bank for a better bank. Open banking also reduced the high cost of entry for new players in the financial services market, resulting in more competition and innovative new products and services. The result has been lower prices and better services in the banking environment.

A 2021 advisory committee recommended to Canada's former finance minister, Bill Morneau, that his government embrace open banking. Three years later, and six years into the successful British launch of open banking, we are still waiting. Banks, of course, favour delay, and the government has been unable to move beyond talking about its plans to actually acting on them.

* * *

Beyond fintech, there is the promise of radical revolutionary change: decentralized finance, or DeFi, facilitated by the rise of cryptocurrencies. The promoters of DeFi claim that it can completely replace centralized finance and the problems it creates.

Part Seven

DeFi is a tech-based, decentralized payments and record-keeping network. Central to its function is the notion of a smart contract which uses computer code to record peer-to-peer transactions to remove the middleman. Records are stored on a blockchain, a decentralized book of record that can be publicly verified, audited, and which cannot be erased. The lifeblood of DeFi is cryptocurrency, which has two essential characteristics of conventional currency—acting as a medium of exchange and a store of value—yet it exists in cyberspace and is controlled by individuals, rather than a central authority.

DeFi promises a farewell to the exorbitant fees, high prices, and customer distress of conventional banking in one fell swoop. Indeed, DeFi, if it delivered on all its promises, would present an existential threat to the banking system as we know it, Canadian banks included.

Banks fear the rise of DeFi not just because it can unbundle individual bank functions, but it can also eliminate the banks' profitable information advantage. The records of Canadian dollar transactions are held on the proprietary ledgers of existing financial institutions, one of the essential functions provided by banks. If you can move record keeping out of the banks to satisfy peer-to-peer transactions, then a big chunk of the banks' economic power is gone.

Harvey et al., in their 2022 book *DeFi and the Future of Finance* are clear proponents of the potential for DeFi to resolve the banking competition-stability-rigidity conundrum. They argue that as DeFi solves the inefficiency problem, it also provides a social service by simultaneously solving inadequate financial access for the poor and economically marginal. Existing fintech has already given birth to micro banking in the emerging world and has ushered in the under-banked and the unbanked to the financial system.

Other claims for DeFi include that it could reinvent the asset management space by creating fractional shares in assets through a process known as tokenization. It may also hold the promise of reducing bank dominance in the management of our investment portfolios at a fraction of the cost.

If DeFi delivers on its many promises, it would be disruptive in a manner unparalleled in history and it would eliminate most, if not all of the consumer pain points discussed in this book. There are problems, however.

DeFi does not do away with the need for regulation, which quickly douses much of the DeFi hype. Regulators will need reassurance before they conclude that it is closing time for bank charters. And that will not be the only source of government resistance.

DeFi's cheerleaders are enthusiastic about the potentials of cryptocurrency, but what gets glossed over in their assertions is what gives the sovereign its leverage over finance: it will only accept payment of taxes in its own currency—in Canada's case, the Canadian dollar. Libertarians like the idea of owning a currency issued in a finite amount *independent* of the need to hold a currency to pay taxes, but they will still have to pay taxes in the currency the tax collector demands. Crypto will not displace the Canadian dollar.

And while DeFi has many purported benefits, it also creates problems of its own, solutions to which begin to look eerily like the problems of conventional finance. For instance, the need to manage the universal financial phenomena of leverage and liquidity which inevitably accompany the provision of financial services.

Creation of leverage can amplify potential gains to investment, but it can also amplify potential losses. Investors that use leverage borrow to buy an asset. If the asset falls in value, then the borrower is at a loss. This might be temporary, so the borrower must keep a stock of unencumbered cash on hand to pay the interest on the debt until the asset recovers. If he can't service the debt, he may have to sell the asset at a loss. This can create systemic settlement problems that can take down the entire financial system, as we saw in the 2008–2009 financial crisis.

Conventional finance participants can minimize the impact of levered losses because they can rely on the central bank to provide emergency liquidity. The architecture of DeFi has many positive features, but its design is incomplete. Lacking a lender of last resort, DeFi resorts to "overcollateralization," or the pledging of more assets than the value of the debt it holds. The excess volatility of cryptocurrencies creates the need for large collateral holdings, undermining the purported cost savings of DeFi.

Persistent cryptocurrency volatility has led to the emergence of stablecoins, a crypto unit that seeks to maintain a fixed exchange rate to, say, the US dollar. Centralized exchanges have been built to facilitate the transactions necessary to reduce price volatility and to survive, DeFi is leaning on the stabilizing institutions and mechanisms of conventional finance. The closer DeFi comes to solving these problems, the more it looks like what it wants to replace.

What's more, DeFi has not yet proven that it can provide a resolution to the trade-off between competition and system stability. During the 2008–2009 financial crisis, banks ceased to lend to one another because of the sheer scale of losses, and no one knew for sure how much loss they would incur. If this had happened under a DeFi regime, the losses would be somewhere in cyberspace, and despite the existence of an accurate decentralized ledger, the work of processing, assigning, and recovering losses in the absence of a centralized network would make regulators uncomfortable. This is not a trivial issue and it suggests DeFi may be less transformative than its cheerleaders suggest.

Things that look too good to be true, usually turn out to be untrue. Igor Makarov and Antoinette Schoar of the London School of Economics argue in a paper for the National Bureau of

Economic Research that despite the promise of DeFi, it is pollyannish to believe that it can be expected to deliver a high degree of disruption. At the core of their criticism is the observation that any financial entity and its supporting infrastructure are prone to concentration to minimize costs, and where there is centralization there is economic power.

As it stands, the complexity of DeFi presents a serious challenge for public acceptance. The trust necessary for widespread public acceptance will be hard to establish without a regulatory seal of approval. Moreover, without good governance, the DeFi revolution is unlikely to succeed.

PART EIGHT

The 2008–2009 global financial crisis shook the world economy to its foundations, taking down some of the biggest names in banking. Overall, Canada had a good crisis. None of our banks went down. They suffered impairment and received some government support, but none required public funds to survive. Losses were relatively small and readily absorbed.

That Canada's banks, generally considered old-fashioned and plodding, not only survived but continued to lend, maintained their profitability and their ability to raise capital, and even paid dividends to shareholders through 2008–2009, made them a curiosity throughout the banking world and a benchmark for good practice and regulation. They were celebrated for opting out of the risky innovation and complex games being played in the world's major financial capitals.

Not all was rosy in the Canadian economy. It went down with every other economy, experiencing a deep recession that required substantial fiscal and monetary support. Because its banks continued to function and its financial infrastructure remained intact, credit and government support were able to flow through the banks to those who needed it, which wasn't the case in either the United States or the United Kingdom. We were spared much pain and anguish.

Most importantly from a political point of view, Canada was spared the ugly politics of bail-outs. Taxpayers were saved from underwriting a potentially expensive and divisive intervention of the sort that roiled other jurisdictions. The populist waves caused by the crisis crashed into American and British institutions but raised barely a ripple in stable Canada.

Characterising the necessary and stabilizing US government intervention as a bail-out was unfortunate, as stabilizing intervention is nearly always profitable. And let's not indulge in any libertarian fantasies that government intervention was unwarranted: during the sweeping crisis, no private lender was prepared to step up and provide the capital necessary to arrest the financial meltdown. Government was the last line of defence, a line that simply could not be abandoned. Handing out a spanking for moral hazard in the depths of the worst crisis since the Great Depression was not the way to go.

The Great Financial Crisis was a twenty-first-century "run on the bank," a contemporary version of an all-but-forgotten predicament where rumours of loan losses threaten a bank's insolvency and see depositors rush to the tellers *en masse* to withdraw their deposits before it is too late. Bank runs were common in the nineteenth and early twentieth centuries, leading to the establishment of deposit insurance and lenders of last resort to stop them. The 2008–2009 crisis was a run on the entire banking system, traceable to poor mortgage underwriting standards and large defaults in the United States. This time, the run was driven not by individual depositors trying to withdraw their cash, but by professionals doing much the same thing in the inter-bank loan market. Banks around the world simply refused to lend to one another, hoarding their cash for fear they wouldn't get it back. The flow of credit froze and blocked the financial plumbing.

Every day, banks trade with each other, placing their excess cash as deposits at another bank that might be short on the necessary deposits to fund its lending. The bank that has surplus cash and the bank that is short on cash might change from day to day, but this market allows the banking system to function. Trading goes on because demands for payments are always met. If there is a shortage of cash for the system, the central bank steps in to make up the difference. If this chain is broken, the whole system can be brought down, hence the term "systemic crisis."

More particularly, the 2008–2009 financial crisis had its roots in the American originate-to-distribute model of mortgage creation. By its rules, a bank would originate mortgages and, once it had a sufficient number of them, pool them and sell them to investors. If a bank is going to hold a mortgage on its balance sheet for thirty years, the bank will want assurance that the mortgagee is willing and able to carry it throughout that time. If the mortgage is only going to be held long enough for it to be securitized in a larger package of mortgages sold to an investor, the bank's need to assess the mortgage's quality is diminished. It's an invitation for banks to write risky mortgages, and in the years before the crisis, they did, accumulating assets of steadily worse quality.

While the originate-to-distribute model got the risk off the banks' balance sheets, the mortgages were not shifted instantaneously. They remained on the balance sheet while they were packaged to be shipped out to investors.

The securitization of mortgages was accompanied by the securitization of other assets, including collateralized debt obligations (CDOs) and collateralized loan obligations (CLOs), often leveraged to boost returns. Infamous CDO-squared deals were assembled—pools of CDOs of mind-boggling complexity designed to obscure and leverage risk, allowing their sponsors to maximize returns while distributing the risk to investors. Much of this activity was accomplished by non-bank players, but it nonetheless had direct links to the banking system.

Financial markets knew that a rot of bad mortgages was festering in the system. But no one knew for sure where they were and which bank was most exposed. Moreover, the growth of credit default insurance, where one party buys insurance against default on their holdings from another party, created a false sense of security. When you write insurance, you create a liability against which you need to hold an asset to cover any necessary insurance payout. However, many entities that wrote credit insurance did not hold assets against the insurance they had written, leaving the buyer of the insurance unprotected.

A 2007 downturn in US housing prices exposed the rot. Mortgages began to default, their losses often amplified by the exotic and complex financial structures in which they were held. Two obscure credit hedge funds sponsored by the French bank Paribas found themselves in a state of illiquidity. This was the first signal that big losses were coming, that they were going to be absorbed by investors, and that a US domestic problem was going to be a global problem. The trust between investors and banks, and the trust among banks themselves, evaporated. That's how the whole system of interbank and wholesale funding markets froze in the summer of 2008. It took the rest of the year to thaw.

The United States lay at the nexus of the financial crisis, and its central bank, the Federal Reserve, was the first and most powerful responder to the emergency. The Fed needed to flow its cash to where it was needed to thaw frozen credit. However, the Fed faced an unanticipated challenge.

In a major difference in economic and financial structure between Canada and the United States, a lot of US financial activity had migrated to "shadow banks," which were financial entities and special purpose vehicles that acted like banks, but were not subject to bank regulation. At one point, the shadow banking system was estimated to be as large as the regulated system. And, as one would expect, risk had migrated to those areas of activity that faced either light regulatory oversight or none at all. The shadow banks, however, relied on the regulated banking system and investors for liquidity, and neither of those sources proved to be reliable in the heat of the crisis.

The Fed learned that it would have to be a banker not only to the banks, which it was established to do, but also to the non-banking entities that would rely on the banking system in normal times. This was a major crisis requiring unorthodox and creative intervention to stabilize, up to and including recapitalization of the entire banking system, with public funds.

Even though the Fed knew what it had to do, it didn't know which financial institutions were in trouble, which needed cash, where they were, and in what legal form they were constituted. It was a wicked problem. Normally, the Fed would lend against government bonds, which have no chance of default. Now it had to take private collateral of uncertain credit quality, exposing itself to potential losses in a way it had never done before.

The scale and scope of US intervention were staggering, something only the state had the resources to accomplish. It injected funds from the US Treasury into thinly capitalized banks as well as shadow banks and stabilized the system. Necessary as it was, the intervention created that lingering impression of rich bankers being bailed out of their bad decisions at the expense of ordinary Americans.

The dominance of Canada's conservative, prudent, and profitable banks meant there were few shadow banks and special purpose vehicles active in Canada in 2008. The overly complex and risky products creating havoc elsewhere did not proliferate here. There were some on the balance sheets of Canadian banks, but not in catastrophic volumes. Neither the Bank of Canada nor the Department of Finance had to engage in rescue operations on quite the same scale and complexity as those in the United States. The Bank of Canada extended substantial operating funds to the banking system for a prolonged period, and the federal government through CMHC bought a significant number of mortgages from the banks to provide them with additional liquidity. But there was no need to extend urgent credit outside of the established banking system.

There is no question that Canada's regulation and supervision of its banks was superior to that of the United States, which paid for its inadequate oversight, as did the rest of the world.

Bank regulation in Canada was and is comparatively rigorous. In addition to clear and well-defined rules, Canada's regulators promote solid principles of financial conduct. As a result, Canada's conservative bank management culture avoids excessive complexity, leverage, and risk, and seeks to ensure that a bank's balance sheet is sufficiently capitalized to withstand shocks. Canada showed the world the scale of capital levels necessary to withstand the ravages of crisis-induced solvency issues. All of this can be traced to Canada's generally more conservative economic culture.

Unlike the United States, Canada's regulation of banks and insurance companies is centralized: the Office of the Superintendent of Financial Institutions closely supervises these institutions and sets their capital requirements. In the period before the financial crisis erupted, OSFI required banks to have a minimum capital equal to 7 percent of the balance sheet in tier-one equity—equity that is unencumbered by an obligation to pay dividends. But this wasn't enough for our cautious banks. They topped up their capital, adding another 2 percent of the balance sheet to hold 9 percent in tier-one common equity, giving them a huge loss-absorbing cushion compared to banks around the world and more than twice the then-inadequate global standards.

There was more. OSFI demanded that overall leverage at banks be constrained to twenty times capital. This was to limit the potential for balance sheet compression due to asset price deflation or defaults that would impair the balance sheet. By contrast, Lehman Brothers, which filed for bankruptcy on September 15, 2008, sparking the brush fire that ignited the full-burn crisis, was levered thirty-three times.

Part Eight

Not only did Canada's banks have substantial capital to absorb potential losses, but they also had a larger proportion of their assets funded by stable, government-insured deposits, meaning that they were less exposed to the drying up of wholesale funding markets. And, because the Canadian banks have lots of rich pickings from their retail customers, they were free of the competitive pressure to shore up profits by innovating and creating the complex products that got the Americans into trouble. Incentives matter. With a domestic business profitable enough to both meet shareholders' expectations and pay for the expensive additional capital, it was little wonder that Canada didn't get out over its skis.

One piece of Canada's regulatory framework did prove inadequate, and that was the provision for liquidity, defined as having (or being able to borrow) cash to meet your obligations. The failure to provide for liquidity can be found at the heart of all financial crises. It is clear from the scale of support from our federal authorities that the banks had not provided enough liquidity for difficult times.

Canada's banks, like their American cousins, relied on wholesale markets to fulfil their short-term needs. That caused them some problems, but the most arresting liquidity event happened in the asset-backed commercial paper market, a form of shadow banking. (Typically, a commercial paper borrower has a stand-by line of credit at a bank just in case the market for short-term borrowing and lending dries up. The borrower can then go to the bank to get by when markets cannot do so. Holders of ABCP got trapped by the issuer's absence of stand-by bank funding and their capital was frozen. It took some time to resolve, and the liquidity hit affected other players in the market.)

Canadian regulation and supervision were clearly incomplete. It took federal intervention to arrange a standstill with investors at home and abroad to manage this situation over many years. Still, our problems were nothing like those in America.

Canada indulged in a bout of self-congratulation following its good financial crisis. Let's not begrudge ourselves at that moment, but from a distance of fifteen years, we might still ask some critical questions about whether the institutional and regulatory beliefs that favour stability over competition are both warranted and acceptable.

We seem to have emerged from the crisis with a sense that competition and liberalization in the US banking sector were responsible for the run on wholesale funding markets that kicked off the crisis. We think that if Canada reduced barriers to entry in its banking sector, allowing new bank competitors to launch and foreign banks to set up shop here, an aggressive rival to the existing banks might pursue lax credit policies, write a lot of bad mortgages to gain market share, and raise the probability of future defaults and potential crises.

None of that holds up to scrutiny. Competition alone was not the cause of fragility in the US banking system. History shows that runs on banks are independent of industrial structure, or where you put your banks on the spectrum between perfect competition and oligopoly. Bank runs are typically a function of poor lending practices. Whether a bank pursues prudent or lax lending practices is a function of leadership, corporate objectives, governance, and close regulatory supervision. These parameters are independent of market concentration. Tolerance of monopoly or quasi-monopoly will not, in and of itself, prevent bad lending and bank runs from happening.

That's not to say that competition, in and of itself, is an incentive to good management and a guarantor of stability. Highly competitive, largely unregulated banking systems have run into grave problems in the past, which is why we now have deposit insurance and an implicit guarantee from governments that some banks are too big to fail—the welfare of the banking system is paramount. Again, banking practice exists on a spectrum between pure competition and super-stable oligopoly. The optimal position avoids both extremes and seeks a balance of competitive pressure with regulation and close supervision.

The problem with Canada's banking system is that we don't see the spectrum. Our politicians and regulators behave as though devolving excessive market power to banks is the sole alternative. We can't get enough stability, and we can't get far enough from real competition. We have convinced ourselves that our only choice is a binary one between an oligopoly and a casino.

The dominant, self-congratulatory narrative on Canadian banking in the wake of the financial crisis is that concentration is a necessary condition for stability. Bank executives love this narrative. The recent crisis gave them a powerful opportunity to play on fears of future crises and encourage Ottawa to double down on profit-stoking stability—and Ottawa listened. Competition-crushing capital requirements for banks went higher still. But the self-congratulatory narrative is not true.

It would be possible to inject more competition into Canadian banking without permitting an over-reliance on exotic, high-risk financial engineering, or without allowing a full-blown shadow-banking system to develop. It would also be possible to regulate and adequately supervise a banking system, providing the public with a reasonable degree of assurance in its stability, without permitting the development of an expensive oligopoly that soaks consumers and drags down our economy.

The question posed by critics of Canada's banking structure, one that fails to receive a straight and defensible answer from either the federal government or the banks themselves, is whether the cost of extreme anti-fragility is acceptable. Increasing discontent and cynicism toward banks among the general public—fed up with the sheer costs of bank services, the unavailability of credit, the miserable rates of return on deposits and investments—suggest that the status quo is *not* acceptable. Yet no one in Ottawa is making the case for reform.

The political defence of the status quo relies on faith in regulation, conservatism, and industrial concentration as justification for inaction, all of it backed by lingering good feelings about Canada avoiding the worst of the 2008–09 financial crisis. But faith is belief held in the absence of evidence, and reliance on one albeit significant historical event to sustain a belief that concentration is a key pillar of stability seems insufficient. There is also plenty of historical evidence that we can have more competition and liberalization if we are prepared to regulate and supervise. Given the emphasis Canada puts on regulation and supervision, and its apparent successes, this suggests we should be able to do a better job of optimizing where we lie on the spectrum between competition and expensive concentration. Yet we continue to scare off calls for a better competitive outcome by positing that the only alternative to our system is the chaos of competition. The argument borders on sophistry.

That Canada got most things right with regard to regulation in the financial crisis should make us more confident, not less, that we can make room for new entrants and establish some competition in the banking sector. We know the challenges to stability new entrants pose, so we can supervise them to minimize the impact of rising default probabilities. Spanish economist Xavier Vives, whose banking system research spans multiple jurisdictions, shows that today's large, complex banks are difficult to understand, increasing the probability of systemic risk. The antidote, however, is not to allow a highly concentrated banking system with barriers to competition. It is to rely on things Canada already has: large capital requirements, leverage caps, and demanding liquidity requirements. These were indeed the key lessons and fixes adopted by regulators around the world in the wake of the financial crisis. Canada had been there all along.

PART NINE

Canada's banks have bedevilled our policy makers for generations. There have been several attempts to spice up competition in the sector, the last major one being the 1964 Royal Commission on Banking and Finance, also known as the Porter Commission. It concluded with recommendations to improve competition in the banking sector by reducing barriers for foreign banks operating in Canada and seeking to level the playing field between banks and trust companies.

There were additional pro-consumer recommendations designed to improve bank services as well as access to banking, especially in rural and underserved areas. Transparency in terms and conditions of financial products and services was emphasized. And, this being Canada, the commission also stressed the need for stronger regulation to ensure the stability of the banking system.

In response to the Porter Commission, changes to the Bank Act were drawn up and introduced in 1967 by the minister of finance as a "blueprint for competition." The changes did help consumers by removing credit quantity restraints and providing better access to residential mortgages, but, as one would expect, it was the commission's emphasis on stability that was taken to heart by politicians, regulators, and the banks themselves.

Jack Mintz, the renowned Canadian economist, president's fellow at the University of Calgary School of Public Policy, and occasional bête noir of our financial industry, penned an exhaustive analysis of the impact of the 1967 changes to the Bank Act. He demonstrated conclusively that compared to the period from 1963 to 1966, the period following enactment of the 1967 reforms saw the after-tax realized rate of return for the chartered banks rise from 7.4 percent to 12.8 percent, a jump of 5.4 percent. In contrast, the same returns for the trusts and loan corporations that the new emphasis on competition was supposed to benefit rose from 9.3 percent to 10.9 percent, a slender gain of 1.6 percent. This observation brought Mintz some rather impolite criticism from at least one bank leader.

A later critique of the post-1967 Bank Act environment by J. W. Dean and Peter Scwindt concluded that the competitive solution sought by the Porter Commission was beyond its grasp, and the banking system remained as concentrated as ever. There were subsequent reforms in the 1980s and 1990s, but they broadened the range of financial services banks could offer and enhanced their ability to merge with or acquire other financial companies. The fundamental un-competitiveness of the banking system persists to this day.

A review of Canadian bank policy was long overdue when the financial crisis hit in 2008–2009. Canada's performance in that crisis confirmed the wisdom of resistance to the global trend toward deregulation that had spread from the United States and was copied around the world starting in the 1970s. Nevertheless, as we've seen, our regulators, encouraged by the self-congratulatory banks, drew the wrong conclusions from the crisis. Canada tilted the balance between market concentration and competition further in favour of the former. This policy preference gave the banks greater power to levy high prices, which was seen as a reasonable price to pay for more stability. However, this assumption proved misguided.

While an uncompetitive banking sector in which a small number of players exercise dominant market power might be a *sufficient* condition for stability, it is not a *necessary* condition for stability.

Part Nine

Canada had a good financial crisis; the equally concentrated Netherlands, Belgium, and the United Kingdom did not. Concentrated banks may be bigger and have diverse lines of business, but they can also assume larger risks. What Canada got right was the strong regulation and oversight of bank capital, leverage, and liquidity. We don't need a concentrated system that confirms massive market power to banks to achieve effective regulatory outcomes.

While we must ask for more efficient, competitive banks, we should be realistic. It is naïve to think that banking is the same as any other sector in the economy and that all we have to do to make it more competitive is to deregulate it—let anyone in, relax capital requirements, embrace high-risk innovation, or permit another shadow-banking colossus to develop. That would be a recipe for disaster.

Regulation and supervision—and particularly large capital requirements, leverage caps, and demanding liquidity requirements—are necessary to ensure the delivery of a reasonable level of financial services while preserving the stability of this critical piece of public infrastructure. There are limits to how far we can favour competition at the expense of stability.

At the same time, it would be a mistake to simply equate the introduction of competition with high-risk deregulation. Competition and deregulation are often conflated, but they are not the same. It is possible to encourage competition with selective deregulation or, to use a better word, *liberalization* of bank policy.

Liberalization is not the same as deregulation. Liberalization means the relaxation of constraints on certain financial activities. It means exposing incumbent banks to competitive pressure from non-bank service providers kept at bay by the delay of Real Time Rail and other barriers to payments system access. It can be combined with new constraints on abusive or anti-competitive activity to deliver a more efficient consumer outcome and, above all, minimize the massive value transfer from consumers to shareholders that currently distinguishes our banking system. This approach would aim both to moderate the behaviour of banks and encourage alternatives through competition to exclude the heavy hand of mandated price controls.

We've seen modest progress in liberalization over the last decade or two in telecommunications—another sector that delivers its shareholders indefensibly high margins for what is essentially a public utility. Ottawa has aggressively encouraged new entrants to improve competition and bring an end to price gouging. It has required the dominant telcos to make their infrastructure available to low-cost providers of wireless, cable, and internet services; de-bundled cable offerings so consumers can pay only for the channels they want; and banned a range of hidden charges and junk fees, such as unlocking fees on mobile devices, among other measures. Our telco sector is still expensive by international standards, but important consumer pain points are being eliminated in spite of official hostility to non-Canadian entrepreneurs who have attempted to bring a measure of competition to the sector and have quit, traumatized by frustration at the state-corporate nexus of non-cooperation.

There are a number of remedies the government might consider for the banking sector. The purpose of this book is to demonstrate the need for reform rather than dictate the manner of reform—any changes would require due consideration and consultation—but the following points give a sense of the range of options available, which might at least spark a conversation.

- Impose on the banks a much stricter duty of care for consumer welfare, one that protects the interests of customers in retail financial markets and enables and encourages them to make better-informed decisions that achieve positive financial outcomes.

Part Nine

- Introduce a New Zealand-style disclosure registry where issuers of financial services must file detailed information beyond basic metrics of financial stability, such as detailed information about their products, including fees and performance, to enhance transparency and investor protection.
- Address the costs of banking services, highlighting the excessive fees and charges from chequing accounts to ATM and foreign exchange transactions. There is no silver bullet here, but *in extremis* fees could be banned or capped; fees could be tied to the service delivery cost, or reduced to a flat fee for all customers, to eliminate price discrimination, among other measures.
- Address interest rates on credit cards by capping rates or linking interest rates to the real cost of credit losses and fraud risk; ban punitive over-charges; encouraging low-cost competitors; and inject radical transparency into the credit card sales process.
- Encourage competition in banking services by mandating low-cost or free access for non-chartered financial service providers to the payment systems and the Interac network; restrict terms on which banks can acquire fintech start-ups and other competitors in the Canadian financial services market.
- Improve the mortgage lending environment by mandating longer-term fixed-rate mortgage options at non-punitive rates; encourage non-bank lenders to enter or expand their business in the mortgage market. More competition may allow us to anticipate less need for (and a lower cost of) CMHC insurance for non-bank lenders.
- Mandate that the big six meet a minimum requirement for lending to small and medium independent businesses—they can afford to share a reasonable amount of the risk inherent in growing the most important sector of our economy (the already high spread incorporates a credit loss premium). Alternatively, they can contribute to a fund that enhances the ability of other

financial service providers to lend to small businesses, perhaps backed by government credit guarantees.
- Impose a stricter fiduciary duty for wealth managers to act in the best interests of their clients; impose stricter disclosure rules around fees, conflicts of interests, and the costs of financial products; require a clear link between benefits received and fees charged in wealth management services; ban commission payments from product providers to advisers so that clients can decide for themselves the value their advisers bring.
- Apply the weight of the Bank of Canada to ensure that our payment system is modernized to serve the best corporate and consumer purposes. It's time to lay down the tracks for Real-Time Rail, even if it means bashing the banks' heads together, as was necessary in upgrading infrastructure for the continuous link settlement system over twenty years ago.

There may even be opportunities to relax what are now unusually high capital requirements and tight leverage ratios for new entrants in the banking sector (we are well above the stringent Basel III international standards introduced after the 2008–2009 crisis, and they are about to become still more onerous, further dampening the availability of credit). This would require tighter supervision by regulators, but so would most of the measures above. Protecting the welfare of consumers in an oligopolistic industry *always* requires more supervision, and Canada falls down on this count.

Our failure to promote competition is evident in government budgets. Canada underspends on its regulation and competition agencies relative to the United Kingdom. In fact, per capita we spend about 19 percent less on regulation and consumer protection and 45 percent less on competitive assessments and investigations. That says a lot about the policy neglect and misplaced priorities of Canada's authorities. Funding and empowering the appropriate agencies—the Competition Bureau, the Office of the Superintendent of Financial Institutions, and the Financial Consumer Agency of Canada—could dramatically improve competition and consumer protection in Canada's banking market while still ensuring stability.

This is a much different approach from conventional deregulation in the shape of fewer rules and constraints on banks, and a reduced intensity of regulatory oversight. Avoiding deregulation that can lead to insufficient bank capital, excessive leverage, and financial crises does not rule out other reforms. Again, what made the US financial crisis so spectacularly destructive in 2008-2009 was a lax regulatory approach to both solvency and liquidity. None of the measures listed earlier would pose the least threat to bank stability.

In the absence of these measures, consumers should do their best to protect themselves from excessive fees and charges on savings accounts and foreign exchange. Lower credit card rates and less expensive investment alternatives are available if you take the time to seek them out. An abundance of information is available online to help consumers search for better deals and develop an analytical framework for better investment choices. Shopping around will offer some protection from the worst banking practices, but nothing is really going to change in Canada's banking environment without a full slate of serious reforms.

Bringing competition into an oligopolistic market is no easy task. It's difficult for the new entrants: They face large fixed infrastructure costs to enter new markets, and they must incur high variable costs as they staff up to provide services. It's also difficult to move consumers to new options. They are accustomed to their current banks, even if they're treated abysmally, and the cost, disruption, and risk of changing brands are scary where your money is involved. New entrants must pay a premium to attract customers.

And the incumbent banks aren't going to sit back and allow a new competitor to siphon off parts of their business; they'll reduce their own prices for as long as it takes to see the competitor off, only to return to the old ways once the threat is banished.

The banks will also spend a fortune on lobbying, whining to Ottawa about the threat to instability and the cost of making crucial infrastructure available to new entrants. They'll dust off their old maxim that Canada's system is expensive because it is safe, and that we should be prepared to pay for it. Canadians and their politicians must counter that our banking system needs to be both safe and affordable. And we'll need to point out the hollowness of that other old banking chestnut that Canada is a small country whose companies need to be big at home in order to compete with larger firms abroad. The fact is they don't bother to seriously compete abroad. Even if they did, there's no reason Canada's consumers should finance it. Banks are here to serve their customers, not the other way around.

It is time Canada's banks were reacquainted with that corporate purpose. The fact is that the banks rent our banking system—this critical piece of public infrastructure—at the public's sufferance, and the public needs some rewards for granting the banks this stewardship. The big six should be ashamed of themselves for milking the Canadian market for equity returns roughly double what they accept in competitive markets, and for delivering fantastic returns to their shareholders and lining the pockets of their executives, who take massive incomes for managing what is essentially a low-risk public utility, all while providing Canadians with inferior and indefensibly expensive service.

This is where our politicians come in. A determined, comprehensive approach to reform is essential, and it won't happen without them showing the backbone to shelter their constituents from the constant storm of bank lobbying. The recent passage

Part Nine

of two major updates of Canada's competition policy (bills C-56 and C-59) has been a major step forward, but, as always, execution is everything. The Competition Bureau needs more resources and the competition commissioner more power to monitor and enforce new competition standards. And our politicians need to muster the commitment and grit to stand behind these authorities, rather than overrule them, as happened in the recent Rogers-Shaw telecommunications merger.

Canada's economic policy makers need to wake up to the fact that they are not the pro-market promoters they think. Rather, they are pro-business advocates. They have consistently put the interests of individual banking firms ahead of those of our financial services market. Promoting mistaken beliefs has allowed economic efficiency to dwindle, and along with it our living standards. Banks have powerful network effects. The choices they make in credit allocation, and the prices and wages they set, cascade throughout the economy. Canada's bank CEOs worry about Canada's appalling productivity performance, yet don't recognize that their own organizations are central to the productivity challenges that bedevil us. We are falling behind the rest of the developed world. It is time to act if we are not to be consigned to the margins of economic progress.

The path is clear. We have to shift our support from regulation that is concerned for stability, and only stability, to regulation that liberalizes markets from the grip of oligopoly and protects the welfare of consumers. We can do it while still allowing the government to keep a tight rein on the solvency and liquidity requirements that help to avert financial crises.

Yes, there would be a lot of hard work and technical hurdles to clear, but we *can* do this. We are good at regulating financial institutions to encourage the behaviour and outcomes we want—we're simply focused on a too narrow set of behaviours and outcomes.

Successful reform of financial services will restore and sustain competitiveness as a complement to solid regulation. It is necessary to lower prices for financial services, improve access to banking, and build greater household wealth. Reform is a fundamental precondition to the more vital small business sector we need to revive Canada's innovation and invention. Only a sweeping reform of our financial services industry can reverse our long-standing trends of mediocre economic growth and productivity declines, and lift all Canadians to a higher standard of living. It is time to demand better.

ABOUT THE AUTHOR

Andrew Spence is an independent financial consultant and economist. Andrew has extensive experience in banking from time spent in Canadian and global banks. He was also an investment executive at two of Canada's largest pension plans and was Special Adviser to the Governor of the Bank of Canada.

GIVE A THOUGHTFUL GIFT

1 YEAR PRINT & DIGITAL SUBSCRIPTION

**SAVE 20% OFF THE $19.95
PER ISSUE COVER PRICE**

- **Four** print books
- **Free** home delivery
- Plus **four** eBooks
- **Free** digital access to all SQ publications
- Automatic renewal

DELIVERY & PAYMENT DETAILS

Subscriber Info

NAME:
ADDRESS:
EMAIL: PHONE:

Payment Options

- Enclose a cheque or money order for $67.99 (includes HST) made out to Sutherland House Inc. Send to Sutherland House, 304-416 Moore Ave, Toronto, ON, Canada M4G 1C9
- Debit my Visa or MasterCard for $67.99 (includes HST)

CARD NUMBER: ____ ____ ____ ____   **CVV:** ___
EXPIRY DATE: __ / __   **AMOUNT:** $
PURCHASER'S NAME: **SIGNATURE:**

OR SUBSCRIBE ONLINE AT SUTHERLANDQUARTERLY.COM